MONTANA TIME

MONTANA TIME

John Barsness

LYONS & BURFORD, PUBLISHERS

10 9 8 7 6 5 4 3 2 1
Printed in the United States of America

Library of Congress Cataloging-in-Publication
Data

Barsness, John.
    Montana time / John Barsness.
        p.   cm.
    ISBN 1-55821-162-4
    1. Trout fishing—Montana.   2. Natural history—
Montana.   I. Title
    SH688.U6B37   1992
    799.1'755—dc20   92-15066
                                                          CIP

Contents

vii

MONTANA TIME

ICE-OUT

Charlie Brown tells us that happiness is a warm
puppy. To this reporter, happiness is a cold
trout.

—ERIC SEVAREID'S
RETIREMENT SPEECH

One December I was in Niagara Falls, which may seem to
be an odd place to travel to from Montana at that time of year,
and is. The wife of a friend, a nice woman from Buffalo, New
York, asked me just what there was to do in the winter "out
there," since we didn't have amenities like shopping malls or
the other cultural attractions of Buffalo.

At the time I was living in a very small ranching community
in the center of Montana. When we first moved there my wife
Eileen asked the very same question, and found that our neighbor, the wife of a retired rancher, painted china in the winter,
something my grandmother used to do after she homesteaded
in the area around the turn of the century. Eileen found that

there was a regular china-painting group, as well as a quilting group, in town. She thought she might do a magazine article on the old crafts, and started asking everybody she met what they did in the winter.

One evening we were shooting pool down at the local saloon (another good winter activity, and one I highly recommend) and started talking to a local rancher. Finally Eileen explained her project and asked him what his wife did in the winter. He scratched the stubble on his chin, took a drink of beer, looked at the ceiling for a moment, and said, "She bitches."

That is certainly a western craft that's been kept alive, especially during cold snaps. It was so cold this morning that the cottontail rabbits living in the chokecherry bushes along the old creek channel didn't get up until around ten-thirty, with the sun high over the snow, pausing every few hops to shake their hind feet. One of them is not a very experienced rabbit: He wandered around in the blue shadows beside the brush when he could have found a small opening in the grass on the hillside below in the sun. That is what the mule deer on the juniper hill beyond do—get up late and sunbathe until the temperature rises to zero—though they also must move at night, to keep the blood flowing, because their hoofprints mark a fresh trail between the house and the barn each morning.

Down in the valley the Missouri River looks like a miniature version of the Arctic icepack, full of three-foot pressure ridges and incipient icebergs created by a few weeks of temperatures that rose above freezing only twice and dropped anywhere from ten above to thirty below at night. Even the goldeneyes and Canada geese have left for warmer places, probably northern Utah, and there's not much to do except cross-country ski in the daytime and put another chunk of lodgepole on the fire at night. It is not a bad time; after the long climbs after elk in November there has to be such a time, to rest and wait for the next year. What makes the wait more pleasant is the sure knowledge that there are indeed cold trout in the river. Very cold trout.

This is part of the world where fly fishermen congregate every year like bears along an Alaskan salmon river to catch trout from famous rivers. Those from the East usually fly in, while those from the West Coast often drive, but they all bring very fine rods and many know an awful lot about catching trout. In restaurants in the evenings you can overhear their conversations, full of big trout and different flies. They probably catch more trout in their week than I catch in a month.

But there is something missing, even in all that fine travel. I know, because I travel myself quite a bit, to catch fish and other things. These anglers are tourists. They don't live here in the winter, and that teaches something about trout, even when not catching them, that all the technical proficiency in the world cannot—especially to those of us who are technically indolent and financially semi-indigent. Instead of forcing yourself to learn, you absorb. You live by the river and feel the changes in it, just as you know without looking at your wife or husband that their mood has changed. You feel the river even at twenty below.

Two weeks ago, when it was thirty below, steam rose from the creek behind our house, from the riffle above the bridge. I'd never noticed it before, perhaps because we'd never gone from such warm to bitter cold so quickly. Then I realized that there must be an underwater spring in that section of the creek keeping the water open. It was not a warm spring—common in this country—otherwise I'd have felt it even through hip boots in summer, but a plain old groundwater spring. In most of western Montana these leave the earth at around fifty-two degrees Fahrenheit (groundwater springs reflect the average year-round surface temperature), and now I know where I can catch trout in extremes, whether in late August or the last week of November.

But even that is a sort of deductive knowledge, though arrived at in a very lazy way; instead of pulling on insulated waders and dipping a thermometer, I looked out the window. Perhaps the ability to feel rivers comes in the same way. Some call it a native intuition, romanticizing it, claiming it belongs only to Inuit and Dakota, the !Kung tribes of the Kalahari Desert, and Australian aborigines, that "we" have lost "it." I don't think so. Fifteen years ago I lived on a Dakota reservation and watched one of the older hunters and fishermen in the tribe find walleye in the rivers and deer and sharp-tailed grouse in the hills. It seemed magical, another sense beyond mine, when he'd one day say, "We're going to the mouth of the Redwater," and we'd go there and catch walleye. Or he'd take me to the badlands west of Blacktail Butte and say that there must be a deer in the big coulee. There would be, and there would also be wild plums near a spring on the north side of the butte, just ripe.

It seemed magic—until after living there several years, through winter and summer, I found myself doing some of the same things, and not just in the places I'd visited with Ben, but places I found myself, and not by random wandering, but by feeling my way into the river or the hills. And then I realized we haven't "lost" what the Dakota and !Kung have; we simply haven't gained those things. A !Kung child opens its eyes in a world where finding water is an absolute necessity; Ben grew up in a country where, if he did not catch a fish or find a deer, his family would not eat, at least at certain times of year.

And so I live by the rivers, putting lodgepole on the fire in winter and trying to catch trout whenever the water shows itself between layers of ice. And sometime in spring—usually in late March or April, but occasionally in February—the chinook winds come from the southwest, the "snow-eater" winds that rise up over the mountains and then gain speed as they fall down the eastern slopes, warming as they fall. Sometimes they blow for a day or two, sometimes for most of a week, but always there's a morning when the smell of last fall's cured grass and this day's wet earth mix with the wind, and you feel the time. You can't book a plane for the date—even if you rushed out here, the day might be gone again before you arrive. You must live here through the winter to feel the morning when you can, once again, catch a cold trout.

Rock Creek is one of the famous streams I prefer to fish at unfamous times. It heads in the Sapphire Mountains of western Montana, flowing into the Clark's Fork of the Columbia, and like many Montana streams flows through a north-south canyon, handy topography for the collection of solar energy. Close to the vernal equinox, sunlight bounces off the snowy rockslides and dark green trees of the Sapphires and warms up the winter-shallow waters of Rock Creek.

You can catch trout all winter in Rock Creek—I once caught one on my way up the canyon to cut a Christmas tree, on a day just above zero, noticing five dark shapes along the shelf ice as I steered the pickup slowly around a snowy bend in the road. There was a fly rod already rigged with a stonefly nymph behind the seat, and I walked carefully out on the ice (which, since it had been twenty below the night before, could have supported several Shiras moose) and cast out into the current, then let the white fly line sweep downstream against the edge of the shelf. I started a hand-twist retrieve and soon felt a light tap, as if someone had set a coffee cup down at the other end of a conference table. At the second tap I raised the rod, and a foot-long brown trout turned once in the bend of the shelf before I knelt and twisted the fly out of his mouth. That was the last day of the season, November 30, but I caught trout in January there, too.

A number of people did, since the stream was open to white-fishing all winter; if you caught a trout you had to release it. In all the years I fished Rock Creek I never saw a winter white-fisherman, with his long bait-pole and mouth full of maggots (this last is not a derogation of whitefishers: a lot of them keep their bait in their mouths where it won't freeze; whitefish have small mouths, so maggots are effective and easy to raise in the winter, unlike earthworms). Instead I saw a very few other people with fly rods catching a few whitefish but mostly catching and releasing trout. This was totally legal, but it made the fish-and-game people nervous, so they opened an official catch-and-release winter season. I still hardly saw anybody.

But January fishing is only quiet desperation. Real fishing usually begins in March, on one of those days you can feel—and now, I realize, that you can see. It was not so much in the air as in the water. I would be walking downtown over one of the bridges to check the mail after my morning class at the university and look down into the Clark Fork. Winter water is clear and black at the same time, almost as opaque and thick as old motor oil under low-solstice sun. It coils rather than curls against concrete pilings, like a rattlesnake caught in the current and pushed downstream around an angler's legs.

And then one day the sun tilts upward and shifts the clouds. The water turns blue, of course, but at the end of a couple days of sun a sheen of green and brown undercuts the blue. The water is still cold as hell, cold enough to numb your hand within half a minute, but the green-brown means the river has slipped out of estivation, that the algae and insects and zoo-plankton have begun to stir. To someone who lives by the river, it vibrates as surely as the wings on a drumming grouse, and means that Geology 302 can do without one particular student for the afternoon.

The bighorn sheep were down by the road, eating first grass along lower Rock Creek. When I parked, windshield into the sun, the pickup's cab grew warmer. Even in the shadow of the topper, as I sat on the tailgate to pull on my waders, the air seemed imported, trucked in from somewhere else—perhaps northern Arizona—to replace the stuff that had hung around gathering woodstove smoke all winter. There were deer tracks in the snow as I walked toward the side channel, narrower and more heart-shaped than the square bighorn prints. The deer would feed earlier in the day and later than the wild sheep; now, at eleven in the morning, they'd be up on the first bench in the timber above the river—probably watching me.

Fishing Rock Creek in early spring is like printing a negative of late July. The whole creek is bounded by very steep moun-tains, but the first six miles or so also contain a flat valley of hay fields and pastures running north and south, fully exposed to the sun all the long solstice days. The creek is always cooler than the river it flows into, too cold to grow really giant trout, but that lower stretch turns a little too warm in August for anything except night fishing. The sun comes off the dark green mountains from six in the morning until after nine at night, and the trout say the hell with it and stay deep until the ridge shadow covers each pool. You work the deep pools at dusk, partly because that is when the trout eat, and partly to avoid all the Californians who've come to fish famous Rock Creek. They go back to their motels an hour before dark.

In March the same hot lower valley gathers all the solar energy possible from the low sun, warming the riffles above the pools. The trout that have held in the pools all winter move up into the lower slots in the riffles, some of them very nice fish of three pounds or so. There are those who never fish this lower stretch, the most accessible from I-90, feeling it doesn't contain many big fish. That is pretty much true until the leaves begin falling from the cottonwoods in late October, by the time all Californians go home and even a graphite fly rod begins to feel more like a .30–06 to most Montanans. When the cottonwoods go bare the browns begin to spawn, running up the creek from the Clark Fork, and some of them stay all winter.

Just for me.

At least that's what it feels like in the first warmth of March. That, perhaps, is the real gut of fishing, once we get beyond the walk-in-the-wild, contemplative-angler stuff we keep extracting from Izaak Walton. When we walk through the rotting snow of the first day of spring, watching the one small herringbone cloud near the mountain edge and feeling the sun warming our right ear just above the collar of our wool jacket, we are some-how certain that it's all for us. For me. Fishing is as selfish as love: Even when you share it with someone you care about, letting that person catch the trout rising in an easy pool, it is just to make you feel good.

And it damn well does.

It felt good to slide down the snowbank to the shelf ice along the big riffle that bends away from the bighorn meadows. The upper crust of the ice held air bubbles trapped as fast water froze in January; almost melted, they felt like eggs popping under the felt soles of my waders. Under the eggshells the rest of the ice was anchored to shallow rocks. At the edge of the ice I knelt, rather like a bull buffalo—the only way you can kneel in cheap chest waders—and pried an unfrozen rock from the stream. Underneath it held the huge green caddis of Rock Creek, and one black salmonfly nymph, *Pteronarcys califor-nica* as the hatch-matchers call him, curling in fright. He, or she, was absolutely black, the length of the first two joints of my little finger. In two months the underside of the thorax would turn salmon as the flies prepared to crawl out of the water and hatch, but for now the nymph was still entirely submarine, a clawless black minilobster. I carefully replaced the rock and whacked my hand against my waders to restore circulation, then took a crude imitation of the black nymph from a fly box and tied it to the nylon monofilament of the fly rod's leader.

This looking at what's under rocks is a very important part of the ritual of fly fishing. I still do it even though for the most part I know exactly what fly I'm going to use long before I stand in the water. Especially on Rock Creek, since I'd spent half a spring there collecting samples for a graduate class I'd somehow talked my way into; the other half I spent in a hot laboratory, picking through jars of silt and bugs, sticking them under a microscope, identifying eighth-inch mayflies by the patterns of their gills, sorting out caddis, trying to pull tiny midges—stickerless midget mosquitoes—out of old mud in one piece. During those months I grew very fond of old *Pteronarcys* and his giant relatives; they came out of the mud whole and huge and honest, like convenience-store robbers taking a step forward out of the police lineup, raising both hands and shouting, "It was me! I done it!"

No, I already knew what bugs lived in Rock Creek, and what the trout ate. But for some trout anglers there's still a need to lift rocks long after they know what's going on, a need that rises from a certain empathy with the quarry. You reach the point where the oozy underside of a wet rock, crawling with off-yellow mayflies, olive caddis worms, and two or three crunchy black salmon flies, begins to look appetizing. Perhaps it's just psychological. After all, if you can look at a squirming green worm and think, "God, what a juicy sucker," then quite probably the trout will, too.

I replaced my hors d'oeuvre rock, tied on my fake *Pteronarcys*, and looked for a place to cast. "Cast" is a loose term when applied to flinging weighted salmon-fly nymphs. The principles of fly casting depend on the fly line weighing more than the fly; ideally, when the line is cast, in the same manner as a mule skinner whipping his whip, the fly follows. Most salmon-fly nymphs have a specific gravity approaching a brick's; though they are not as big, the aerodynamics are the same. Casting a *Pteronarcys* resembles the delicate art of dry-fly casting (or mule skinning) in the same way tossing the caber resembles a curveball.

I looked around for some place to toss my caber. Perhaps eighteen feet from the edge of the shoreline ice shelf, a two-foot rock barely broke the surface of the riffle. Behind the rock the current had excavated a little hole, perhaps shin deep. Despite the sun's warming effect on the riffle, the water was still in the forties, and a cold-blooded trout wouldn't have enough energy to fight the full current. So I started false-casting, ducking my head as the salmon fly went by the first time, and when I'd worked out enough line I leaned into the rod and let the fly go. The heavy rod (you need a big rod for *Pteronarcys* in the winter) bent and then straightened, and for a pausing instant I felt like I was pole-vaulting upside down.

The nymph landed a foot short of the rock. The yellow fly line swept past and downstream in liquid parabolas, and I concentrated on the tip. This is the center of nymph fishing, the line tip. When properly greased, it floats. Water makes it float in predictable ways. If it floats weirdly, you assume a trout has glommed onto your fly and lift the rod and pull on the line, trying to hook the fish.

On this cast the fly line did nothing weird until it drifted down below the rock, when three or four inches of the tip eased sideways against the blue-brown water and I struck savagely, the only way to strike on the first fish of spring. Unfortunately this was not a fish but a rock, and my salmon fly came out of the water and hit me on the left nostril, right where a pimple was forming. It hurt but was not permanent, so I cast again.

On the second cast the fly line did nothing weird, but one of the bow-waves of the rock did. It suddenly humped up like a bucking horse and I recognized the side of a brown trout inside the wave. It was more bronze than brown and moved differently than the water, vibrating for a moment inside the wave and then wedging sideways and slightly upstream as it disappeared. The sight of the trout brought on another persistent thought:

There really is a fish in this river.

Nymph fishing is predicated on a faith as blind as a blank piece of paper. It is not like summer fishing, where you can often see fish rising all over the damn place. Until you see or turn or hook a trout when nymphing, you could be starting all over again, at the beginning of trout time, waiting for something very much like Godot.

The hard and elemental beauty of the fish I'd just turned (it indisputably had emerged from behind the rock to look at my fly, I said three times to myself) was that I hadn't felt it. It had never taken the fly, and would undoubtedly whack my *Pteronarcys* if I put it anywhere near the rock again.

So I did, bending forward like a heron in the shallows as the line floated over the riffle, the unseen monofilament and black nymph down behind the rock. My pulse rate rose and even my numbing feet, welded to the ice, remembered they had nerve ends. When the tip of the line took a sudden surge directly toward the rock, I pulled down hard on the fly line with my left hand and raised the long rod high with my right, the fish feeling as if I'd hooked a rock-wave, a hard compact turn. I saw the dorsal of the brown, too, just before the six-pound tippet popped.

It is very hard to break a six-pound tippet on a two-pound fish, especially when nymph fishing, because of all the slack line in the water. It is the angling equivalent of leaning a dull knife into some nicely sauced beef and watching the meat whirl across the table onto your dinner companion's white dress.

Except that in late winter there's usually no one around to see it. Some wise person once said that what you do when alone tells the truth about your ethics. It also tells the truth about your vanity. I cussed. I cussed not just my muscular reflexes but fly fishing itself.

And then I tied on another tippet and another salmon fly, and cast again. I cast two or three times to the hole behind the rock, hoping the brown would strike again and I'd catch both him and my intricate nymph, the product of a half-hour at the tying vise. But it was a hopeless hope and I knew it, and soon my cold feet and winter vaulting pole were off in search of someplace new.

I never really understood biblical references to swaddling clothes until I started fly fishing in winter. In three to four layers of wool, flannel, and rubber, searches for new fishing never go far. Mercifully, after January and February they do not have to—everything looks good. The next hole appeared perhaps thirty yards upstream along a dead log. This time I had to wade, since the log was anchored too far out in the stream for me to cast a weighted salmon-fly nymph with anything short of a crossbow. Say forty feet.

I eased into the water like a frail old man. Even as a student of biology and geology, I was never really convinced that crude oil came from ancient vegetation until I waded Rock Creek. Its rocks (oddly enough, it is aptly named; there are hundreds of Fish Creeks, Bear Creeks, and Sixmile Creeks in the West where you'll never catch a fish, see a bear, or be six miles from anywhere) are the slimiest things this side of Prince William Sound, even in late winter with the aquatic biota at low ebb. It is the one Montana stream that really deserves wading cleats, but poor college students do not buy wading cleats for one stream. Consequently, my Rock Creek technique was to worm my toes under the large rocks, looking for firm footing like an old man testing his balance with every step. This I did, eyes on the log.

After a dozen steps the log came slightly closer. Guessing I was in range, I false-cast three times, then let fly the *Pteronarcys*. It landed twenty feet short. This is about par for chicken Rock Creek wading. I wiggled ten feet closer and tried again, knowing I was still too far away. And I was right. It may seem odd to be so cautious in eight inches of water, but on slimy rocks the very shallowness becomes a hazard. Instead of drowning, you dislocate knees or break bones. I've waded winter pools in the Bitterroot that came within three inches of my wader tops and felt much safer—an illusion, because if you go under in forty-degree water, you're not likely to come up again.

The last ten feet in the middle of the channel took as many minutes to cover; the faster water had swept away all but the biggest rocks and any sort of foothold was scarce. I pressed the tip of the fly rod into the water downstream for balance, and even then almost shattered my kneecap as a big trout, for some goddamn reason hiding in that fast water, zipped upstream from behind a rock—the rock I was attempting to squeeze my foot behind. It looked like a rainbow. I don't know what else would care to hold in that current.

Aside from me, of course.

At last, anchored in a defensive posture resembling basic aikido, I cast. The first cast was once more slightly short, but only because I was trying not to fall. The second reached the head of the log, but without enough slack in the fly line, and the current pulled the nymph out of the slow water before it could sink to trout depth. I stripped in the line and looked again.

Two problems: A branch from the log, leaning into the stream in the perfect place to cast the fly; and the current alongside the hole, so fast it pulled the fly line downstream and the fly out of the hole. The ideal casting position would be five feet closer and three feet downstream; from there a slack cast upstream would drift perfectly into the trout's world with only a couple of feet of fly line on the water, not enough to drag the fly into the main current. But two big rocks blocked the way, big enough that I'd have to step over them. There might be sure footing on the other side, and there might not. If not, I'd surely scare any trout in the hole.

So the correct cast was from where I stood. I looked at the branch, at where the water swirled along its base. The grain turned gracefully there, at the creek's surface, where a cotton-wood twig tried to escape the eddy created by the branch. That was where the cast should land. I let out line again, false-cast three times, and then let the fly go, this time with thought.

It landed right there—on top of the branch. I tried to ease it over the edged grain, and the hook tip caught in the wood. I raised the rod, hoping to rip the fly out, and it sunk deeper.

I dropped my hands to my side, barely holding the rod. Why hadn't I taken up radio-controlled model airplanes? I looked far away, at anything but the branch, and noticed the bighorn sheep feeding their way up the snowy mountain, precisely visible even at a quarter-mile in the hard light. And then I noticed for the first time that their horns curved in the same segmented half-coil of a drifting *Pteronarcys*.

I breathed again and broke off the fly. The tippet did not

break off this time, and I thanked the deity of chance for that as I tied on another salmon fly.

Stripping line out again, I took an offensive stance—not of war, but of entry. Instead of regarding the log as an obstacle, I perceived it as the backdrop of my perfect cast: Without the branch, the cast could not be perfect, for there would only be open river. I looked at the imprisoned cottonwood twig, false-cast once, and let the fly go.

It landed just beyond the twig, the tippet dragging one end of the twig under the surface as the heavy fly sank. The twig tilted, then slid from under the nylon, out of the eddy, and floated downstream along the log. I leaned forward, holding the rod toward the log, left hand against the lowest rod guide waiting to take up slack, and noticed a dull flame in the black water, like one turn of a bronze gong in a dim room, and almost struck. But my mind said that the fly line was still three feet above that flash, that the fish had turned to investigate the floating twig, and I waited. The line drifted, then moved a sudden inch toward the log, and I lifted the rod and pulled the line past my waist. The gong turned again, higher in the water, and I felt the fish, as if the river had decided to fold in on itself and take the fly line with it.

The fish ran back under the log, and I tilted sideways, rod parallel to the water, and held the rod there as the fish held hard in the dark hole. It could not hold long in the cold water, and quickly turned out into the current and then downstream into the fast rocks below me. I held the rod high and let the trout swim in hard angles against the tall bend—I could see it was a trout now, a brown, the red points on its side the red of winter, as if the cold shrunk them into smaller, denser particles of color. The trout's head angled more and more toward mid-current, toward me, and then I reeled the slack in, holding it against the cork grip until the line was on the reel. Then I reeled even faster, bringing the rod up, and the trout's head came up and he planed on his side into the water below my knees. He was just broad enough for my fingers to ease under his belly and my thumb to flatten his dorsal fin as I held him over the surface, almost-invisible scales breaking the light down along his side. I held the rod in my teeth and twisted the big fly out of his jaw, then bent a little more—not defensive or offensive now, just there, in the water—and held him under the surface, head upstream, and opened my hand. He held there for one gulp of airy current, appearing under the surface to be the same metallic brown of the water. And then he disappeared into the black hole again, almost before I realized I'd caught and held the first cold trout of spring.

Rubber Pants and Shallow Water

> The artificial fly is not necessarily a sporting
> gesture, even though it usually is. There was an
> ego-crushing salutation of a Colorado resort
> owner of thirty years ago.
>
> "Fishing is so good now," he said, "that you
> won't have to use those flies. The trout will bite
> on worms!"
>
> —CHARLES WATERMAN,
> *A History of Angling*

Voices carry—over calm lakes as clearly as through a Walkman, so as I stood in twenty-eight inches of water along the shore of the reservoir I could hear every word from the large woman in the boat that trolled a hundred yards from shore. Her mouth ran as steadily as the five-horse Evinrude on the back of the boat. Her husband, a thin, sallow man who needed a shave, ran the motor and nodded about as often as he changed course—just often enough to keep her mouth going, and to keep from running aground.

Her commentary was distinguished by its smoothness, a stream of consciousness that took in the raft of coots down the lake ("Look at that bunch of ducks out there. Why I would've thought they'd still be south . . . "), the success of other anglers, both on shore and in other boats ("He's got another one, Fred, why aren't we catching any? Maybe we should try over there, at least to see what he's using. Maybe . . . ") and the contents of the lunch box at her feet ("You want another cookie Fred? There's potato chips. That Coke didn't set well this time of day, maybe I'll have some chocolate milk . . . "). It did not take long to find me.

"Look there, Fred. That guy's walking in the water. That must be cold. Why didn't he just bring a lawn chair like everyone else? Oh, he's one of those fly fishers. Look at that, Fred, that's kind of pretty, the way he casts. Oh, he got it caught in one of the willows. If that's what happens, I don't know why they bother. And wading in that cold water . . . " (Here she paused to reach down over the side to dip a finger in the still lake.) "Oooo! That is cold! Hey, he's caught a fish. Probably a sucker over there in that shallow water. 'Course, maybe he's from back East and don't know any better, hey, Fred?" (Fred nodded.) "But why's he in the water? Oh, look Fred, he's wearing rubber pants. That's how he can walk in that cold water. Look at that, Fred! He's lettin' his fish go! Now why would he catch suckers and let 'em go? I have half a mind to tell the fish'n'game. Of course they wouldn't ever . . . "

Her voice faded as the boat putted around the bend of the

shore. Perhaps Fred took her over to look at what the other boats were catching them on. I kept catching trout, for that is what the fish were: rainbow trout enjoying the warm shallow water in that never-never land between trollers and lawn chairs.

The average western angler has three pieces of equipment, all geared to an either/or outing (either the fish bite, or they don't). One, a spinning rod; two, a boat or lawn chair; three, a cooler. In the first days of spring, these are brought to a lake rather than a river because rivers move. There is nothing so upsetting to a weekend angler who has just endured two months of mud as something that moves, especially with mud in it—and that defines western rivers in May. These gentle folk want instead something that rests quietly in front of them—or under their slowly moving boat—while they dangle a bait of garlic-flavored cheese, or troll an orange-and-gold lure. If a trout bites, fine. If not, a day sitting by (or on) the lake is better than staring at the TV and letting the kids and dog track mud through the halls.

On one Saturday my wife and I arrived at the local lake with nonstandard gear. We brought a fly rod and a pair of insulated chest waders, and a chocolate Labrador retriever puppy. He went off to play with some children and dogs while my wife pulled on the chest waders and I tied an olive Woolly Worm on the leader of the fly rod. We both got done about the same time, and I handed her the rod. I sat on a stump on the beach while she carefully waded out as far as she could without shipping water, perhaps fifty feet from shore. She false-cast a number of times, only dropping the fly onto the water on her backcast twice. This was not bad for a beginning fly fisher, and soon she cast out about thirty-five feet and began stripping in the fly, slowly and steadily. A wave came up behind the fly, and I said, "There's one." She struck just before the trout did, the fly line landing around her shoulders like a toga, except not so flat and manageable.

"Damn!" Eileen said, and picked the line up from behind her ear.

"Wait until you feel one. Then raise the rod." I was looking down the shore at the puppy as he played with a little girl. He would run up to her as fast as he could, then slam on the brakes (hard for a forty-pound puppy), and then reach out gently and flick her nose with his tongue. She'd scream and giggle and he'd head out for another run.

"Thanks," Eileen said, with little grace, and cast again, with a little more. In two more casts another trout followed. This time she waited and raised the rod after the fish turned. He jumped immediately, pink side precisely visible when he paused, as straight as a steel hammer, before falling back.

"What do I do now?" Eileen asked.

"Let him run. Let the line go under your fingers."

So she did, and the rainbow ran fifty feet out into the lake and jumped again, not quite so high. She played him closer, and then he ran again, not so far. She began backing into the bank, leading the fish. I stood and walked down and knelt in the shallows, cradling the fish in my left hand and turning the hook out with my right.

"Catch another," I said.

"All right," she said, and smiled. She did, too, about five minutes later. This one, not quite as big, jumped too, and as soon as she felt in control of the jumping trout she looked over and said, "This is fun."

I nodded.

The line of lawn-chair anglers down the bank had also taken notice, since garlic-cheese bait was evidently not part of the food chain of the day. A lanky guy in his mid-forties finally got up and came dawdling down the beach. He stood a few feet away from me and we nodded to each other. I had just unhooked Eileen's second fish and she was carefully wading back into casting position. He looked at her, chest waders up to her armpits and the lake almost up there too.

"Gettin' pretty serious, isn't she?" he said.

I nodded. "Yes, she is."

He watched as she cast. Then she hooked another trout. I went down to unhook it and when I returned to my stump he had headed back to the line of lawn chairs. When he got there, instead of sitting down he stood and cast. Then the guy next to him, perhaps his son, did the same. Soon two-thirds of the people along that section of shoreline were standing. Evidently that was our secret.

Ten minutes later they were all sitting again. Eileen had caught another trout, making it four, and her arms were getting tired. As we walked back up to our pickup, calling the brown puppy, they looked at us oddly. Maybe the secret was the rubber pants.

Well, yeah.

The ice goes out on the lakes later than on the rivers, in the valleys sometime in late April. One spring we went to a mountain lake that still had very thin and rotten ice hanging along the shorelines, and the larger cutthroats we caught would run back under the shelf, the tippet cutting the ice in quick jerks, like someone ripping up old linoleum.

But that is equivalent to catching river trout in January. The real fishing begins around May first, which is a very good thing indeed, because that's about the time the spring rivers rise and turn to mud. The real fishing is something like bonefishing in a land of snowy mountains, the Bahamas less thirty-five degrees.

Bonefish are caught on "flats," the shallowest parts of the shoal waters of islands in tropical seas. Bonefish flats are so shallow they're often dry at low tide; when the tide floods these little bays and inlets, bonefish follow from deeper water to feed on shellfish. Some flats are better on an incoming tide, others on an outgoing. An extended bonefish expedition develops its own circadian rhythms, as different from the rhythms of Eastern standard time as ragtime from a metronome. You cease to sleep and eat according to clocks, instead living on the syncopation of the moon and tides. Walking around in warm salt water seems normal. You hunt the flats (for that is what bonefishing is, hunting more than fishing) as the next step up on the food chain. Bonefish follow shrimp, you follow bonefish. Life becomes that simple—and complex, for the flats do not flood in exactly the same rhythms every day, the ease of water changed by moon and wind, and the flat where the big fish come each afternoon for two days can be empty the third.

The early lakes are like that, but built on annual rather than diurnal rhythms. Even the color of the water is a darker version of the same luminous Caribbean green, limestone marl mixed with glacial silt, and big trout come up on flats—though it is the time of year and not the tides that brings them. The first time I found them was in a shallow lake in a big sagebrush valley just west of the continental divide. Local fly-fishing rumors said there were big rainbows there, so I went, a backpacking stove and tent in the Bronco just in case the fishing was good.

The lake was twenty-five miles of gravel from the highway, then another five of plain dirt. If it weren't for the surrounding mountains wearing the long level slice of last night's snow, it could have been a five-hundred-acre mud puddle in the Great American Desert. There was a peninsula jutting into the middle, with two outhouses surrounded by a dozen vehicles with boat trailers. Most of the boats were out trolling. I got out to stretch and see what was happening. In thirty minutes one boat caught a foot-long trout. This didn't seem promising, so I went for a drive around the lake.

The dirt track was full of miniature lakes and needed four-wheel-drive in some places. Along the eastern shore the water was very shallow, the bottom made of gravel the size of Bartlett pears, washed clean by waves created by the prevailing westerlies. Driving slowly through two long parallel mud puddles, I gazed at the shallow green water and noticed a school of fish.

The school milled in water that looked not more than a foot deep, the closest fish perhaps thirty feet from shore. As soon as the Bronco reached dry land, I braked and got out and walked over there.

They were trout.

They were rainbow trout, the smallest a foot and a half long, a couple of pounds, the largest over two feet. The closest moved off when I walked slowly up to the bank, but most of the twenty-odd fish milled slowly, a middling cast from shore. Then I saw a broad-backed trout turn on its side and vibrate violently against the gravel, like a fresh-caught tuna dropped on the deck of a fishing boat. And then a very lean, hook-jawed trout chased another through the middle of the school. They were spawning.

Rainbow spawning on lake gravel is the trout equivalent of the rhythm method, though much more certain. Without flowing, aerated water the eggs don't hatch. But that didn't occur to me at the moment. What occurred to me was getting my fly rod.

In western lakes a #8 olive Woolly Worm is never a mistake. I tied one on a fairly heavy tippet, pulled on hip boots, then eased into the water fifty yards down the shoreline from the milling trout. Even with polarized sunglasses and the sun behind me I couldn't see many actual trout, but the water was so shallow—a few inches deeper than a foot—that I could keep track of the more aggressive males by the V-waves they made when chasing other males. These curved in ellipses from the center of the trout school, the bigger males chasing smaller ones outward, then returning more slowly toward the orgy's center.

So I cast along the edge of the V-waves and slowly stripped in the fly. Nothing. I cast again and a wake detached itself from the center and followed the fly. I kept stripping. The wake kept following, then speeded up, and the dorsal of the fish showed along the surface. *Jaws* in miniature. I saw the pink mouth open and lifted the rod, feeling the point of the hook scrape along the trout's jaw. The trout swirled and a V-wave headed back toward the school.

The second follow came five minutes later. This time I waited until I could see the side of the trout when it turned, metallic maroon in the water.

It felt as if I were standing on a third-story balcony holding a fly rod attached to a cowboy boot that had just fallen off the balcony rail. There was a quick and inevitable surge of weight, then a heavy bounce as the trout turned sideways against the rod, and finally a series of lighter bounces as the fish angled back toward the other trout. Some scattered, V-waves fighting one another on the surface, but others just kept on doing what they were doing.

The water was too cold for the big trout to jump, but he tried, rolling several times. This tired him and soon I had the line on the reel and pumped him gently away from the other trout. As he came nearer I could see that it was indeed a he, a spawned-out male turned dark maroon and silver-black. The male trout's color changes as the fat under its skin is metabolized—they live off it while spawning—and different chemical compounds are released. The fat is heaviest along the flank and belly, the reason male brook trout turn the color of maple leaves when they spawn in autumn. The color of leaves and fish is the same because the compound responsible is the same: the carotene that makes carrots orange. Pacific salmon (and rainbow trout, it has been decided, are a species of Pacific salmon) turn red and then very dark in the decadence of spawning. The energy lost is so great that most species die afterward. Rainbows don't necessarily, but often do.

Which is why I did not feel particularly guilty, after reeling him into my net, about carrying him to shore and whacking him on the back of the skull with a large chunk of dry gravel. He was close to two feet long, and even after not eating for a while still so muscular that I couldn't quite get my hand around him and had to brace him against the canvas top of my hipboot. I thought of my bonefishing friend, a sophisticated Florida redneck named Jim Conley who talks about "titty bream"—panfish so broad "you have to hold 'em against your titty to unhook 'em."

The trout shivered and died and I took him down the shore a

ways to clean him, stripping the guts and gills out and tossing them out into the lake. A gull appeared and dove for them. There hadn't been a gull within sight before.

His flesh was as red-orange as a pomegranate and would taste almost as sweet. It seemed too vital next to the decadent dark skin. His belly skin was crisscrossed with gravel spawning scars, like a wooden canoe taken down too many shallow rivers.

When I had him clean and rinsed I put him on the ice in the cooler and then caught some more trout. They still milled out there. Later I would dig out a thermometer to see if there was some temperature change, perhaps a spring hole, that attracted them to that particular spot, for it seemed identical to the half-mile of shoreline surrounding it. But for now I just caught fish.

The next was a female, not as long as the male but heavier. She spilled orange eggs as I cradled her in the net and took out the hook. I released her and the several others I caught, having enough trout for a couple of meals in the cooler. While I fished I noticed a pickup parking a quarter-mile down the shore, and two men starting to fly fish. After a while one hooked a trout and I reeled in and walked down there.

There were two anglers, an older man in his sixties and a bearded fellow in his forties. The older man had the trout on the bank by the time I walked up, a male that looked a little bigger than any of the fish I'd caught, maybe four and a half pounds. He was laying down his rod and taking a penknife out of his pocket. He opened the knife and bent over the fish, sticking the little blade into the vertebrae behind the neck. The trout quivered and then relaxed. The approach was different but the results the same.

"Nice fish," I said. I can always come up with a opening like that.

"Yes, he is," the man said. He had his collar buttoned all the way up and the skin of his leathery neck hung over the button. He smiled. "A neighbor of mine is an old Norwegian woman who likes fish. I normally don't kill trout."

I shrugged. I am a young Norwegian man who releases almost all the trout I catch, but if there is something wrong with killing and eating fish there is something wrong with the natural world. The catch-and-release ethic was developed to protect places where trout can be killed too rapidly to be replaced by reproduction, such as certain hard-fished streams in the East, native cutthroat streams in the West, or Arctic lakes where fish grow so slowly that a big lake trout is over fifty years old.

But the conscious ethic has become an unthinking religion. An acquaintance of mine came back from Mexico one year with a story of how he'd converted a poor peon to catch-and-release fishing on a remote mountain lake. The lake was so full of largemouth bass they'd ceased to grow; there simply wasn't enough food for all the fish. He'd caught and released over fifty small bass in front of his Mexican guide, whose protein for the week was pinto beans and corn tortillas. This strikes me as approximately civilized as the European settlers in Africa who denied the natives permission to hunt because they would only eat the game. True civilization, on our crowded planet, should mean knowing what the land can afford.

Most of the streams in Montana, biologists have found, provide angling just as fine when a few fish are kept as when every trout is released. If you prefer your protein (animal or vegetable) grown with diesel fuel and fertilizer, shipped with more diesel and wrapped in polymers, fine. I'll take at least some of mine directly from the water where it was grown.

The leather-faced angler cleaned his trout by the side of the lake and two gulls appeared. One caught the gills out of the air when the man tossed them. He rinsed the trout carefully and put it in the cooler in the back of his pickup, then rinsed his hands in the lake before picking up his rod again. It was a very nice graphite rod, and he cast it so precisely that his right wrist seemed to move with the absolute minimum energy needed, like the fingers of a good guitar player. He stood on a hummock of new grass along the shore and the line angled out behind him in a fast and straight line, pausing for a brief time before angling down in front of him, just above the water, and then back and up again. He false-cast three times and then let the line go. It curled out over the lake and he bent forward slightly, a pred- atory genuflection, as it settled onto the water. He paused, allowing the fly to sink, then brought it back in a quick hand- twist, the line gathering into his left hand as precisely as hay into a baler. And then he had another fish.

This one was even bigger. I saw it roll on the surface once and guessed it must weigh six pounds or more, and he lifted the rod and set the hook. The fish ran to the right and then angled toward him, the tippet leaving a tiny V-wave, as if a water skipper had decided to ski across the surface. He reeled in quickly and had just gotten the slack fly line on the reel when the fish turned again toward the middle of the lake and the tippet popped.

He stripped in the line, then tilted his head to look at me. "That was a big trout." I nodded. "A very big trout." I nodded again. "Oh, well. I was going to let him go anyway. But I wish I had my fly back. Let me show you one."

I walked over as he tucked the rod under one arm and took a small fly box from his vest. As he opened the box I noticed he was missing half the little finger on his left hand. The fly resembled my crude olive Woolly Worm in size and color, but instead of being a sixty-second dash with chenille and feathers, was a precise imitation of a *Gammarus* scud, the underwater amphipod known to many anglers as "freshwater shrimp." This one, though made of feathers and thread, could have incited lust in another *Gammarus*.

"Very nice," I said. I was full of insight.

"Thank you," he said. "It takes about half an hour to tie each one. Here, take one." He held the fly out.

"No," I said, backing away slightly. "I have something that works. But thanks very much." I knew that I'd lose his fly on the second cast. That is the way the world functions.

By that time it was midafternoon. I walked back down the shore to my personal trout school and found that about half the fish had disappeared, probably into deeper water. I fished for a while longer, catching one more smallish trout, and as the sun angled downward learned my second lesson of the rainbow flats: Spring trout are more active in midday. This ranks right up there with the discovery that fire is hot. Trout are cold. They function best when the water temperature is in the high fifties or low sixties. I dipped a thermometer into the lake. Even in the shallows it was only fifty-two. These trout were not about to eat olive Woolly Worms—or, probably, shrimp scampi—unless· the sun was up high.

So I made my camp on an old river terrace above the lake, built a fire, and broiled part of my trout, seasoning it with fresh lime and pepper. It tasted much like fresh salmon. I read a book for a while until the sun went down, and then went to sleep.

In the morning the immutable laws of cold trout hadn't changed. I shivered into my stiff hip boots and fished until close to ten o'clock before getting a hit. No trout showed where the school milled the day before until noon. Finally I decided I'd had enough fun and went home.

Since then flats trout have appeared on other lakes, at about the same time of year—the first week of May. They appear on the shallow gravelly waters off points, or on sunken bars, anywhere the water is at most two feet deep. Sometimes they come to the same place each year, and sometimes they must be hunted like bonefish. Their rhythms don't shift with the moon but rather the seasons, the amount of snow and cold and meltwater that flows into the lakes, and spring winds. Toward the middle of the month they ease back into the deep black water of the lakes and don't come back again for another few weeks, when the damselflies start hatching. But that is after the rivers fall.

◢◣◢◣◢◣ Salmon Flies
And Other Floating
Objects

Nature is like an enormous restaurant.
WOODY ALLEN,
Love and Death

There had been a thunderstorm the evening before. Fresh deer tracks marked the path through the wild roses down to the river, so many that I felt curiously claustrophobic, as if standing in line at a Moscow supermarket. Nearer the river I found where they'd eaten the tender seeds off some new sweetgrass, the stems smelling faintly of mown hay. Along the bank were the anthropoid prints of raccoon and the empty pieces of a crayfish exoskeleton. I could imagine him down there in the moonlight, hands busy, literally shucking off the crawdad's mortal coil, leaving it here by the bank. If nature is a restaurant, this was an all-night diner.

I looked at the water. This is something floaters do before putting in. Some of it is practical, a check of the path and the river's level to see if any sand bars have appeared during runoff. But it is also something that is simply done: You must see the river.

The water was the color of a murky emerald, traces of sediment suspended in the current. Turning around, I could see the faint dry mud line where runoff had peaked, two weeks before, a few inches up the rose bushes. They were blooming now, full of pink flowers and large insects.

There was a salmon fly on the rose bush nearest my knees, not moving in the morning chill. I reached out and picked it up by the folded wings, turning it upside down to see the color of what one of my dead professors would've called the "ventral thorax." The belly. It resembled the color we call salmon, but seemed more nearly the color of carotene, the orange of maple leaf and brook trout belly and Bugs Bunny's favorite food.

Replacing the salmon fly on his or her bush, I noticed a few tan and empty exoskeletons on other roses and willows and rocks, mortal coils shucked off the day before. Instead of ending up in a raccoon, however, the salmon flies that left these husks were huddled on the roses—or inside a trout.

My wife was growing impatient with my river-looking, calling from the top of the bank that she had all her stuff in the boat. So I hiked up and we walked it down through the roses, angled oars thumping the bottom slightly with each step.

We slid the boat in the water and arranged things quickly— rods and nets and life vests. I sat at the oars and Eileen pushed off, stepping lightly into the bow. The keel touched gravel with her weight, but I leaned back and gave the oars a pull and then we were free.

That is it: Free. The bank eased back like someone walking away, and I pulled hard on the right oar to get us pointed downstream, the boat coming around in the slow eddy below a big rock, and we were free of the earth for at least six hours. The white sun angled above the steep barren hills, illuminating our side of the river with that peculiar dry light of western valleys, a light made of high thin air, its shadows cut in angles by river terraces that rise like curved steps toward mountains. On the other side of the river the hills lay in those blue shadows. Looking in that direction, I saw a few salmon flies flying in the light, seeming the size of sparrows against the dark blue hills. I set the boat thirty feet from the bank, shipped the oars, and picked up a rod. The first cast was a little short, but the second landed near the willows, and a trout came up and slapped at it, like a bear trying to pin a salmon to gravel. Breakfast at the diner. For at least that moment I was grateful that the winter had been a dry one, keeping the river low, though I knew it would get too low later on.

It is a sad fact that Rocky Mountain rivers turn to mud in the spring. Winter can be forgiven—a good time to tie flies, and at least the water stays low and clear, if sometimes very hard. But whose idea was spring runoff? It's like a ninety-minute rain delay in the third inning, the temporary end of stream fishing just when life is looking up. Just how temporary depends on many factors: the warmth of spring, depth of snow, spring rains. Runoff can be over by early June—or last into late July.

Another often-sad fact is that the salmon-fly hatch begins

about this time. The giant *Pteronarcys* nymphs live in streams for two to four years, crawling rather clumsily around the bottoms of large rocks, growing and shedding exoskeletons, before heading to shore and their brief moment of glory, both personal (for sex) and cultural (as objects of fly-angler adoration). They climb up on streamside rocks and willows and shuck off their skins, then fly off to mate and then lay their eggs. They are supposed to lay their eggs in the river, naturally, but will mistake rainy pavement for a river's surface. This may not seem terribly bright but they evolved back when small pterodactyls were the main insect concern.

This tendency was cited as an argument against paving the mostly gravel Rock Creek road, a suggestion made and argued and rejected every few years. One of the anti-paving faction (a fly fisherman) suggested that thousands of female *Pteronarcys* would die under Firestones and Goodyears on rainy evenings, threatening the hatch, as well as anglers whose vehicles might skid off the slippery salmon-fly carcasses into swollen Rock Creek. A non-angler who lived up the creek suggested that this might be a very good thing.

When the salmon flies hatch, traffic goes faster. There are many theories of salmon-fly technique, one of the oldest being to "find the head of the hatch." The hatch is triggered in part by water temperature. The valley waters warm first, and the hatch starts there—the lower portions of Rock Creek, the Madison, Big Hole, Gallatin, *et al.* As weather and water warm, the hatch progresses upstream.

Though the hatch only moves up, traffic goes both ways. The idea is to find the area where trout have dimly realized that large edible objects float constantly overhead—but before the fish are too full to eat. This involves driving upstream and down, watching for airborne salmon flies. Considerable fossil fuel is expended in the effort, especially on weekends. It is hard to drive fast while looking for insects. The roads are often narrow and winding. There are some casualties.

Sometimes looking for hungry fish is wasted effort. Trout eat salmon flies until they puke. I once caught a two-pound brown so full that salmon-fly legs, some still wiggling, protruded from his gill covers. The hatch goes in fits and starts, and not all of a stretch's salmon flies come off at any given time. Spring holes, creek mouths, and shady cliffs keep the temperature down on certain stretches, where the flies can come off a week later, while everybody is twenty miles upstream at "the head." After the hatch some big fish will still rise, hungry again. I usually just find a place to fish and do it, always a more pleasant occupation than driving dusty roads full of temporary sociopaths.

In terms of numbers of trout, the "best" fishing comes just before the hatch when the nymphs start moving, when on good days almost any large black nymph will catch dozens. But the semi-cheap thrill of the salmon-fly hatch is having big fish come up to eat big flies. Just one three-pounder rolling up top beats the hell out of half a dozen fish eating nymphs. Would you rather make love six times while wearing flannel pajamas with the lights out, or once buck naked in an upstairs bedroom on Saturday afternoon?

Since trout hang out under the bank, looking for the first live flies to drop off the rocks and willows, they can be caught right there. Some anglers fish only there, wading directly upstream along the bank, in or out of the water according to depth. Trouble is, anyone can do this, and the foot traffic gets crowded.

It can even get crowded fishing the other way, by floating.

Easily floated stretches of the famous rivers sometimes need yellow lines and yield signs. I have never witnessed a fistfight on an early Big Hole morning at the boat ramp near Divide, but expect to. It would be pretty easy to get onto the water before anyone else—just get up at four o'clock and do it—but the salmon flies don't fly before the sun warms the water. (Many visiting "dude" anglers don't either, having spent too much time at the saloon in Divide the night before, and three-fourths of the boats floating that Maiden Canyon stretch from Divide to Melrose are rowed by outfitters and guides, not local anglers.)

Most outfitters favor McKenzie River-style drift boats these days, a matter as much of marketing as of practicalities. A lot of dudes won't fish with an outfitter who doesn't have a drift boat, regarding rubber rafts or, heaven forbid, johnboats, as unprofessional, something like muggers using screwdrivers instead of real switchblades. It's a matter of style.

But there are real advantages to McKenzie boats. They have deeply rockered hulls, the bow and stern pointing up in the air like a croissant on its side, and high, outsloping gunwales. Only a third of the boat actually sits in the water; a twist of the oars turns one almost as swiftly as a revolving door. Even the worst caster can be quickly positioned in easy range.

The rockered hull also makes McKenzies comfortable casting platforms: The angler stands in the bow to cast, his knees braced in a couple of cutouts on the front of the bow seat, high above the river. (This is also stylish. A lot of anglers imagine they cut a very rakish figure up there, in their Patagonia shirts and new cowboy hats. And it works both ways—as one outfitter said, "I don't lose as many dudes overboard since I started runnin' drift boats.")

On the debit side, the high hull was primarily designed for heavy waves. The original McKenzie River boats imitated surf dories, for work on the big waves of coastal rivers. Most Montana trout rivers are devoid of significant waves, but do have wind. The high sides of a drift boat act like sails in a good Madison River breeze. An upstream wind can literally blow a McKenzie back up the river, and even a downstream wind can be bad.

Eileen and I floated the lower Madison late one May with outfitter and friend Bill DeShaw, of Three Forks. The wind came down the canyon so hard that on a couple of occasions Bill had to get out and dig his wader heels into the gravel. There was no way to row with any control, and we'd soon have smacked a boulder. I'd been casting before the gust came up and still had forty-five feet of #8 fly line out, equipped with a black Woolly Bugger larger than some mice. The wind whipped the line downstream over the water, the Bugger hanging out there like Dagwood onto the last bus's door. When the wind dropped from fifty miles per hour to maybe forty, the fly dipped down toward the water and slapped the surface. On the fourth slap a trout slashed at it.

"Did you see that?" I shouted at Bill, who was holding the boat in one hand and his hat in the other. He shouted something that sounded like, "Catch him!" so I did, dropping the rod tip until the fly bounced on the surface. It only took two slaps for the fish to come up again, a brown of about fourteen inches. There was no problem setting the hook since there's no slack in a fly line at forty miles per hour.

In a wind like that any boat is helpless, but even a normal afternoon breeze makes a McKenzie unwieldy. And they are heavy. This limits launching sites, and I used to fish with a spacy friend who had a fiberglass McKenzie that must have weighed six or seven hundred pounds, at least, loaded up with gear. He always had these great floats he wanted to go on, but never could remember which channel ran free. It is not much fun to float down a half-mile channel to find an eight-foot irrigation dam at the other end. On that occasion we ended up dragging that goddamn boat over a two-foot dead cotton-wood tree.

Another time we floated the Big Hole above Divide, from Wise River down. He acted like he'd done this before but I began to have my doubts. We passed under a bridge toward evening and just as we floated underneath I looked up and saw a sign that said, "GO NO FURTHER OR YOU WILL FLOAT OVER A BIG DAM AND DIE." At least that's what I re-member. So we rowed for shore and made it—unluckily the wrong shore, since the dirt takeout was on the other side. So we got back in and rowed like hell across the river, making the opposite shore a little ways above the dam but several hundred yards of steep willow bank below the takeout. So we dragged that hulk up there, slipping over rocks and twisting our ankles and smashing our shins, wondering how Lewis and Clark's men did this for hundreds of miles—but then again they weren't hauling fiberglass McKenzie boats. Then his little car wouldn't haul the boat and trailer up the dirt slope, so we ended up using a come-along to slowly winch the trailer up the hill, a foot at a time. We winched until well past sunset, when the Big Hole mosquitoes came out. They are famous and should be. I think that was the last time I floated with him.

Some of the same launching and wind problems affect rubber rafts, though they're enough lighter to be launched other places. Some floaters, particularly old-timers, use johnboats, perhaps the most sensible western float boat, more aero-dynamic than either rafts or drift boats, stable with their flat bottoms, and light enough to be carried, both down to the water and in back of a pickup truck, so you can float stretches not blessed with trailer sites—and zillions of drift boats.

Canoes, for the most part, make romantic but lousy river-fishing craft, since if big enough to hold three anglers and gear, they're too big to be fully controlled by one paddler, at least on fast western rivers. So the anglers on each end have to paddle, while the guy in the middle tries to cast while sitting down, adventurous for the paddlers who not only get to watch for rocks but flying Woolly Buggers.

But my own float boat is a canoe, one of those crude Cole-mans. Aluminum-framed and polymer-skinned, it makes a lousy canoe but a great rowboat, thanks to an aluminum rowing frame made many years ago by a Canadian from Vancouver named Lorne Hodgins. He was trying to market the things, and had even talked to Coleman about it. They clamp to the gun-wales with a couple of wing nuts and provide a rubberized canvas seat, two rowlocks, and a couple of rod holders. Lorne claimed he fished Vancouver Bay in his Coleman, catching big king salmon on rods held in the holders. I tried to interest various magazine editors in stories on making canoes into really good fishing boats, but they all yawned. Sorry, Lorne—but your frame works great.

A rowed canoe doesn't turn quite as quickly as a drift boat or rubber raft, or carry quite as much gear, but it does carry an oarsperson and two anglers and enough stuff, and can be rowed upstream in fairly fast currents, handy for fishing or retrieving snagged flies. And it can be carried almost anywhere, so I float stretches unknown to most guides. Once, too, the wind came up so hard we couldn't float anywhere, even upstream—so we picked up the canoe and dragged it across an alfalfa field for three-quarters of a mile to the highway.

Just having a boat, however, does not mean anything. As poor Mole learned from Rat in *The Wind in the Willows*, it is not quite so easy as it looks. Since a western boatman isn't usually confronted by really fast water, the actual rowing is pretty easy. Two main rules cover it.

One: Keep to the main channel. This is mostly a matter of following the flat-water V down through shallow riffles. The downstream-pointing V shows where the deepest water flows, often a matter of eight inches versus five, enough to keep a flat-bottomed boat afloat instead of hanging up or scraping bottom. At islands take the channel with the most water. Sometimes there'll be a logjam or dam to be portaged, but not too often. On the popular floating rivers, like the Big Hole, Madison, and Big Horn, you only have to watch for occasional boulders.

Two: Keep the bow pointed where you *don't* want to go. The easiest control of a float-fishing craft involves back-ferrying—rowing backwards. The current will try to drive you into the outside of bends; keep the boat angled slightly away from the bank, and back-dip the oars occasionally. Sometimes a slight drop-off creates a back current that tries to suck you back toward the drop-off. In this case twist the oars hard to turn directly away from the lip as soon as you drop over.

It isn't hard. What *can* be hard for some people is doing all this while keeping anglers in range of trout water. I've fished with several anglers, including one guide, whose idea was to row down the edge of the main current and let the anglers fend for themselves. This is easiest on the arms and back but doesn't produce many fish; the good places are too far away or go by too quickly.

A good example is the pool below a crossriver gravel bar. The current always finds at least one breach in the bar, and the boat pretty much has to go there. But below the bar there's a deep pool carved by dropping water, with eddies on each side of the main current. Trout love these places because they gather both food and oxygen from the falling water. They deserve several casts, and it's easy to do—the oarsman just has to back-ferry at an angle into the slack water on either side once the boat drops over the bar. Once in the slack the boat can easily be held there by a little oar work. The same can be done in the slack below islands.

The so-called guide I floated with always just sailed right through those places. I got one long cast at each eddy and didn't have time to let the fly work long enough. After about the third time this happened I was going to say something when he commented that I should be casting less and leaving my fly in the water more. I almost wrapped the fly line around his head.

Many rowers aren't aware of when their anglers are straining their casts. The sweet spot is usually along the bank, and the boat should be within thirty or at most forty feet to allow easy casting. Just a few feet more and not only does the casting become strained but the fly isn't on the water as much because the anglers have to false-cast more for distance. A good boat-man is always aware of all this. There's no way the boat can be in perfect position for both front and rear casters all the time, but should be most of the time. The boatman can make the difference between catching ten fish or thirty; in fact, position is often as important as exact fly pattern.

Which is why I rowed that salmon-fly-cool morning. Though I had plans to get her behind the oars for a while, Eileen has never mastered rowing, wingshooting, or fly casting. That's fine, because I know her well enough to realize she'll master what she wants to. She's a fine big-game hunter, photographer, and spin-fisher, things she decided to do. I never urged her to do any of it, which may be why she decided to do them. And why she comes along.

In the first pull of the oars I realized another reason I like a canoe: It floats high and long, like the salmon fly. Out in the current it put us where we were turned and jiggled and pulled, just slightly erratically, like a giant insect. Unlike a McKenzie boat, which despite its turning radius floats more like a log than an insect, a canoe floats with something resembling surface tension, and like a salmon fly floating high on six legs, I felt the ripples of the river under my feet through the polymer exoskeleton, the oars exploring out to either side like antennae. Pausing between pulls I felt even more, as if floating high and weightless on the surface of the river were a sort of Braille, the waves decipherable symbols of the bottom, where trout live.

Eileen's first cast landed a little short, maybe five feet from the willow bank, and on her second cast she cast two-handed, using her left hand on the bottom of the grip to give the spinning rod something extra, and her salmon fly—a real adult salmon fly impaled on a #4 bait-holder hook with a small split shot a foot above the hook—arced farther on the second cast.

She turned the reel handle to close the bail and then waited, easing the rod tip higher as the salmon fly sank, until she felt the split shot tapping the river bottom's rocks, and reeled in again for another cast, looking downstream for the next good place. Float fishing with a spinning rod can be more difficult than with a fly rod—you only get one chance at each eddy or rock, then have to reel in again to cast, instead of just lifting the fly line off the water and, with one backcast, rolling the fly into the same place, or another a dozen feet downstream.

She opened the bail and held the line in her finger, and the next trout place appeared, a boulder next to the bank with a wagon-wheel-size eddy behind it. She lifted the rod, almost touching her forehead, and cast, the salmon fly and split shot bouncing off the side of the rock into the near edge of the wagon wheel. Then she closed the bail and raised the rod, waiting.

"Good cast," I said, leaning hard on the oars to hold us beside the eddy. "Something lives there."

Something did. The bait swept halfway around the eddy and the rod tip quivered once, like the top of a serviceberry branch when a chickadee lands. Then the tip dipped very definitely, and she raised the rod a little more and a trout jumped along the lower edge of the eddy, as if spun out by the whirl. It jumped again out in the river current.

"Rainbow," I said, seeing the red of his side, like pewter washed with thin blood.

She nodded. "He's a nice one." She turned and grinned. "Nice fish." This was a semiprivate joke, begun one fall at an elk camp, a bunch of hunters discussing TV fishing shows—the kind where the host stands in a boat, the camera providing a close look at his down-slanting line and an expanse of empty water, and repeats, "Nice fish," too many times. "Nice fish" became the camp's password. It got so bad that when one of the hunters came back with a spike elk in his truck, another leaned over the edge of the pickup bed and said, "Nice fish." Someone else said, "God, look at all those elk-hair caddises."

This nice fish did not want to come to our canoe. After the first two jumps he angled downstream in front of the boat, leading us around a small midstream boulder. Then we entered a shallow riffle and I dug the oars into the gravel and stopped the boat. The trout tired about this time, his runs slowly zigzagging up to the canoe, where Eileen leaned with the net.

Then she had him, a red-sided trout so broad she could barely get her hand around him as she reached into the green net. "You want to eat him?" she asked. The big hook hung off the edge of his lower jaw. That's the reason we use them; they hardly ever hook gills or throat, as even a fly occasionally does.

I shook my head. "There's more browns than rainbows here. Let him go." So she did, easing the net back into the fast airy water, twisting the hook out with her other hand. She held the net there, letting the current wash through his gills until he splashed hard, then tilted the net forward. He swam in place, nothing in front of him except open river, resting again, gill covers pumping like hinges. Even from my angle I could occasionally see the red of gills behind the hinges—and then he was gone. I felt the urge to blink, as if in closing my eyes I could still see him leaving, like a light trace under my eyelids.

The riffle was a midstream gravel bar dropping off on each side into a channel. I grabbed the bowline and eased out of the canoe, holding the gunwale with my right hand until I could wind the line around a small boulder. We both got out and I rebaited Eileen's hook with a salmon fly from the jarful we'd collected on the bank. She does not like baiting hooks, though she actually enjoys field dressing deer or elk. Go figure.

We each waded to one side of the bar. I took the side toward the blue hills, shadow-line edging the deeper water. Starting at the head of the bar, I cast upstream at an angle, keeping the deer-hair salmon fly just on the edge of live water, where the diamond-backed riffle met smoother deep water. After every three or four casts I'd take a step downstream and cast again.

And then something took my eyes to the bank, forty feet away across the current. A big rock lay almost hidden by the willows, flat-topped as if inviting an angler to step up there and lower a salmon fly—genuine or ersatz—to the river. It was the rock where I'd hooked my biggest trout, almost twenty years before.

Like Eileen, I was fishing with live salmon flies back then, the way many native Montana anglers fished the hatch, having just been introduced to the method by an older friend. We were camped up the gravel road on that side of the river, and after supper we decided to fish until dark. Back then you couldn't fish later than half an hour after sunset. Who knows why?

The water was typically high that year, up in the willow roots, not opaque but not clear either. Toward dusk it didn't matter; you couldn't see into the water at all, just along the bronzed surface, and couldn't wade because of the speed and depth. So you stood in the thick willows and threaded the rod between them until the bait hung above the water and let the line go, feeling rather than seeing the river.

Feeling the split shot tap and slither through the rocks, my mind worked hard to imagine the world down there, a place not totally unfamiliar. During the heat of late summer I'd snorkeled rivers, scared trout and suckers and whitefish as my long pale shape swam through their private eddies, forced my buoyancy down to the bottom of deep pools to bring rocks to the surface, turning their silted bottoms to the sun to see if any strange deep-water creatures lived there, a nautilus or coelacanth of the Rockies—but finding only the same folks that lived under rocks and silt along the shore: caddis, stonefly, mayfly, cranefly, midge.

Sometimes I'd float, dead-drifting just under the surface, letting the current take me, the fish along the bottom more accepting when I didn't move my arms or legs. Occasionally they edged out of their dark green holes as I passed, but more often just flared their gills slightly—unless my shadow touched them. Then their shadows angled in quick precise vectors across the riverbed, like green spheres across a rough billiard table. It took some time before I could see trout from above, their backs green like the algae and moss of the bottom. But then I recognized motion, separated a small brook trout from tendrils of algae by the way his body did not quite follow the current, despite the camouflage of his green-wormed back.

There were fish in places I never expected, but though I learned some things, there was a barrier between the trout and me more definite than between water and air: my size. Range scientists speak of microclimate, that inch or two just above the soil where grass and twigs and root tops create a different world, moister and darker and calmer than the windy place where huge things live, cattle and coyote and human and pronghorn. It exists along the bottom of rivers as well, stones

breaking the current into shadowed microangles, where caddisflies graze on algae like prairie dogs graze on grama grass,
and salmon flies eat caddisflies like bullsnakes eat prairie dogs,
and trout—like red-tailed hawks—prey on anything alive and
smaller than themselves, caddis or stonefly or crayfish.

Like Alice after eating the cake that made her larger, I could
never enter those dark crevices—unless I baited a hook,
pinched a split shot to my line, and let it drift along the bottom.
Bait is a connection with rivers that no other method of angling
quite reaches. We are visual animals; although we use all our
senses to some extent, we depend more on sight than on the
others and create many of our greatest pleasures around it—
painting and writing, for instance—but even arts involving
other senses, such as food, must please our eyes as well or are
rejected before they're tasted. Dry-fly fishing is a visual art,
predicated on seeing trout take the fly.

But to really know rivers, other senses come into play. Bait
fishing allows us to see through touch, like a coyote sees through
his nose. It is something too many fly fishers never find, always
having their flies and their noses up in the strong current
where anything can float: canoes and logs and even a very
large Alice.

So I bait-fished along the willows on that evening twenty
years ago, looking for places to enter the peach-leaf willows and
put my bait in the river. There was a gap where deer had come
down to drink (I could still see one, a white-rumped mule deer
doe, standing in the yucca and sage on the hill above), a deer-
wide gap in the willows where I leaned the rod out and dipped
my bait in the water. It tapped twice along the bottom and a
fish grabbed it. I raised the rod, hauling the fish wiggling above

the willows and dropped it back in the grass, a brown trout about a foot long, then unhooked the trout and even then, those long years ago, returned it to the river.

Then I found the rock. The backside was almost hidden by tall grass. I tapped the grass with my rod tip, listening for the buzz of rattlesnake, but at that time of evening they'd likely be farther up the hill in the rocks. They were. I stepped up on the rock and eased forward. The rock pointed like the bow of a boat, three feet into the river, breaking the current. I opened the reel and flipped the bait slightly upstream, letting out line with my finger until I felt the bottom tapping through the nylon and fiberglass. Then I closed the bail and let the bait drift past the bow of the stone boat, where it stopped, along the edge of the broken current. I raised the rod and the bait didn't move, hooked on a willow root down there. I reeled in line and stepped forward, then tilted the rod upstream and leaned back, hoping to free the bait. The river bottom moved.

It didn't jerk or thrash or jump, it just moved downstream and angled in toward the bank behind the breakwater of the rock. Then it stopped and I could feel a heavy rhythm, like a panting Labrador retriever leaning against my leg. I was eighteen years old, a fisherman as new as the spring grass behind me, and concrete notions like line strength and reel drag hadn't been entered in the computer. My total knowledge of fishing consisted of realizing there was a big trout on my line.

So I leaned back on the rod. It was sunset, warm light on the water, and a broad metallic orange muscle rolled on the river's surface, as if a bodybuilder had flexed his shoulder under a wave. The muscle flexed once like that, a curving bronze, showing a fin along one edge. Then it dove slowly and turned downstream. I leaned harder on the rod and heard a small crack and then a subliminal hum as the line tightened, and then the rod came back and hit me across my upper lip and the side of my nose. Where a half-second before there had been a live and concentrated struggle there was only an empty river, the sun finally down over the sage hills and the water turning from bronze to something very much like a flat tin roof under a heavy rain, though much quieter, as quiet as a breeze in peach-leaf willows.

And that was the same rock across from me now with the sun rising behind the hills. It was the very end of morning, the last edge of night on the air, sagebrush still smellable in the coolness and red-winged blackbirds talking in territorial imperatives in the willows. This was the time to catch a big trout from alongside that rock, with the bank still in shadow and me still believing. That is what learning with bait gives the fly fisherman: a belief, because he knows the bottom of the river as well as the surface.

The deer-hair salmon fly on my tippet was greased with silicone to keep it dry and floating, and it would have to sink to find a big trout, so I bit the nylon off and tied on another, ungreased, fly, then bent down and held it in the fast water of the riffle, rubbing the hair between my fingers until it soaked up the water. Then I eased forward into the edge of the deeper water and started casting.

It would be a tough cast—not to reach the rock, only forty feet away, but to allow the fly to sink before the current between the rock and me sucked the line downstream, and the fly away from the rock. I false-cast twice, not wanting to dry the fly, keeping the line very high and the loop open and lazy, and

then ended the cast high in the air, the line sailing up over the
bankside willows and then bouncing back, falling to the water
in long rattlesnake curves.

Too short. The fly landed three feet from the rock, out in the
main current. I stripped it in and soaked it again, then bent a
tiny split shot to the tippet, a foot up from the fly. This made
casting clumsier but the final back-bounce of line not quite as
necessary. The line bounced and the tippet and fly fell in a pile
on the downstream side of the rock, the fly whirling for a
moment on the surface of the eddy before tilting straight up
and then disappearing, like a miniature version of the *Pequod*
under the pull of the split shot. The current pulled the line
downstream, straightening the rattlesnake curves, and just as it
started to pull the fly from the eddy I felt a pluck on the line,
like someone snapping a rubber band, and lifted the rod hard,
pulling on the line to get the slack out.

A trout came whirling through the air, a trout slightly larger
than a dollar cigar, parting from the big fly somewhere in the
first four feet of his flight. Both trout and fly landed in the river
in little splashes. Half the line landed on my shoulders.

I tried it again, of course, after deciphering the creative new
knots in the line, but caught nothing. The sun angled up and
took the cool smells of willow and sage from the air, and then
while changing flies I heard Eileen shout and turned downstream to see her at the tail of the riffle, rod bending in short
hesitant surges. As I walked nearer through the shallow water I
could see the reflection of the riffle coming up off the water and
under the shadow of her hat, dancing across her face like the
unfocused light of a large prism.

"Nice fish," she said. And it was, a brown trout this time,

with red spots scattered across his side like puncture wounds that never bled. We kept him for supper, cleaning him along the edge of the riffle and putting him on ice in the cooler behind the rowing frame.

"You want to row for a while?" I asked while rinsing my hands in the river.

She looked downstream. "It looks pretty open."

"It is, and straight. There's a few small boulders but nothing serious."

She sighed. "Okay." She didn't want to, but has an Irish Catholic sense that every moment of pleasure in life is paid for somehow, and payment might as well be voluntary.

So we rearranged the fishing gear and she got in, testing the oars, and I pushed off. She remembered which oar to pull to turn us downstream, and then we were free again. The salmon flies were really flying now, visible all along the bank, especially against the dark shadows at the base of the willows, and I kept putting my fly there, letting it float for a few feet, then lifting the rod slowly until I could feel surface tension pull on the line—then lifting it fast and shooting the line up and into the air behind me like a mule skinner, pausing, then rolling the cast forward again, the line unfolding slightly downstream from the canoe, to let the boat pivot around the fly caught in the slower water along the bank.

On the sixth or seventh cast a trout came up and took the fly. I could see the fly sitting there, like a sailboat almost tilted to the water, and then there was a curve with a fin on its edge and the fly was gone. I was just floating along, casting rather automatically, enjoying the riverbank while not rowing, and there was too much slack in the line. When the trout rose it took a moment for me to realize that, yes indeed, this is what we'd come for, and to raise the rod very high and strip line as fast as possible into the bottom of the boat. Luckily, the trout had taken the fly and mistaken the crisp deer hair for crunchy salmon-fly wings and simply swum back down to the bottom with the fly still in its mouth, holding it just long enough for me to catch up. At the end of the third quick strip of line I felt the trout, something I hope I never live long enough to quite expect.

This was another good brown, jumping once as soon as he felt the hook and then pulling hard under water downstream. Eileen said, "What should I do?"

I looked away from the orange line angling into the water ahead of us, and said, "You could pull up on that sandbar at the bottom of this run." I pointed. I looked at her and grinned. "Nice fish."

So she did, back-ferrying across the current at an angle and easing the canoe up very softly on the sand. As soon as we touched I got out, holding the rod high in my right hand, and held the boat with my left while she got out and dragged it onto the sand. Then I let go and turned to walk up the bank, and saw the startled faces of an older couple picnicking on the sandbar on a grassy flat tucked into the line of willows.

Then I turned to the trout again. He held angling away from me down at the tail of the run, head into the current like a sailboat tacking into the breeze. The six-pound tippet was too light to bring him up the run, and he was too far downstream for me to pressure him much from the side, so I waded down along the sandbar into water up to my knees until the fly line was perpendicular to the current. Behind me I could hear

Eileen starting to talk to the picnickers. The trout held in the current until I could pressure him with the rod held low and sideways. Once his head turned his body lost its bite on the water and he turned and ran out of the current into the pool below the sandbar, where I knew I had him. I saw him near the surface in the still water, the biggest fish we'd hooked all morning, shaking his head, jaws like an osprey's, and then he turned and dove into the dark green water and the fly pulled out.

A collective moan came from behind me. I turned and walked up the bank, reeling in the fly line, Eileen standing in her blue denim jacket and the couple sitting beside their picnic blanket.

"Hello," I said, smiling a very small smile.

The woman shook her head, looking at the pool. She was wearing a frayed straw hat that had a piece of green translucent plastic along the front of the brim. It made her face appear as if it were under water. "That looked like a nice one," she said.

I shook my head too. "It was." I checked the hook. The point was still there, and sharp. I shrugged. "Sometimes that happens."

The man grunted. He had on a new baseball cap that said "Dam(n) Engineers, Not Rivers." He nodded to the pool and said, "Brown?" I nodded, and he nodded back, thinking. "I remember when there were hardly any browns in this river, when it was almost all rainbows and there were even quite a few cutthroat left. That was before it got so warm in the summer."

I nodded again. "It's almost all browns now. Eileen caught one rainbow this morning, a big one. We let him go."

"Good. I should have done more of that back then, but we never thought it would change. Kept everything we caught, except the little ones. We thought that was the thing to do. Pretty soon there were nothing but little ones." He laughed. "You using a Sofa Pillow?"

I shook my head. "No, but something like it." I opened a fly box and picked one out. "This."

He reached up and took the fly. It had a dyed-orange deer-hair body tied on a #8 hook with four big stiff hackles wound over the front half of the hook and a flat wing of undyed deer hair extended back behind the hook. "That looks good," he said. "Tied it yourself?"

I nodded. "I'm not too good, but they work. I stole the idea from someone else. It seems to help a little, the hackle holding the front half of the fly up, like a real salmon fly, the way they angle up on their legs."

"It's a good idea," he said. "Of course, sometimes about anything works this time of year. I run into guys all the time, claim they've invented the best salmon-fly pattern ever. There must be six on each block."

I laughed. "I know what you mean. Probably everything was tried thirty years ago."

His wife looked at the canoe. "How does that work? I've never seen one like that."

Eileen said, "It works fine. Even I can row it."

The man leaned back, holding one knee with his clasped hands, looking over the river. "We used to have a wooden johnboat. It was a good boat, but awful heavy. And I finally ran over one too many boulders. I said the hell with it, and just wade now. Some of those drift boats have been going by. They look awful heavy too."

I nodded. "They are. But they're nice to fish from."

"I bet, especially if you have someone else to row." He grinned. "My father was a chemistry professor at the U. He always said that one of the basic laws of physics is that they're all good fishing boats if someone else is behind the oars."

We all laughed, even the woman, who must have heard the story a hundred times. She turned and looked at her husband as if they were both twenty-five.

"I kept my yearly fish this morning. You want to see him?" the man asked.

"Sure."

He eased to his feet, a little stiff, and led us back to the shadows along the willows to a large metal cooler. He lifted the top and stepped back, motioning us up. Lying on the ice between some cheddar cheese and a home-canned jar of bread and butter pickles was a brown trout. His nose almost touched one end of the cooler and his tail curled up a couple inches at the other. I breathed out slowly.

"I don't keep many anymore," the man said. "I allow myself one like that a year. I know I could just take a picture but there's never anyone along. She doesn't like to wade anymore. And we both like to eat them."

"One will never hurt anything. Did you catch him on top?"

The man nodded. "At the head of the run here, right next to the willows. He jumped once. Then he headed downstream, like yours, and I only fell once chasing him down. Went over my waders, but I'm almost dry now. I was lucky; the hook didn't pull out. I thought it would, when he got below me."

"He's beautiful," Eileen said, touching the trout's side. Then she walked back to the woman and started talking.

The man looked at the fish. "I know I should have let him go, but it's hard to change. I guess I feel I've changed enough in other ways. I got my engineering degree at the U and built dams."

I looked at his hat and smiled. "You don't now."

He shook his head. "Not hardly. I wish we could get rid of the dam on this river. It's what makes the water so warm later on."

I nodded. "It'll silt in. In another hundred years it'll be marsh, and the river'll be cool again."

"Oh, I know. It would be better for you and me, though, to blow the thing up right now. Then we'd see a lot more trout like that one." He nodded toward the cooler. "Though to most people, a trout isn't much. I learned that living in California. To them, a river is something to build a freeway over, so they can cut twenty minutes off their commute." He smiled a very thin smile. "I built some bridges, too."

I shrugged, wanting to say something that would make him feel better, but not having much faith that anything would change myself. Most people do not like rivers, or anything else that won't entertain them while they sit down.

"Well, good luck," I said. "We have to get down the river if we want to be off by dark."

"Good luck to you, too," the man said, extending his hand. His palm had surprising strength, and yet held my smaller hand precisely. I wondered if that came from the drafting table, or days with a fly rod. "Land the next one. And let him go."

"I'll try."

Eileen was talking antique quilts intently with the woman, so I rearranged the canoe so I could row again. She came over as I finished. "I had my chance," I said. "It's your turn again."

"Okay," she said lightly, the voice of someone who has done her oar penance.

I sat in the frame and she pushed off, the bow leaving a groove in the sandbar between the footprints. The man and woman waved from shore as I pulled on the oars. "Good luck again," the man said, lifting his voice above the wind in the willows. I waved back, not saying anything, free again. Or at least as free as we ever get. The river only flows one way.

▲▲▲▲ CUTTHROAT AND GRAYLING

> She was thinking. I could see, even on that
> short acquaintance, that thinking was always
> going to be a bother to her.
>
> RAYMOND CHANDLER,
> *The Big Sleep*

In many years spring runoff washes out the salmon-fly hatch, at least for fly-fishing purposes, even on the upstream reaches of the famous rivers. One year it snowed all April and rained all May and June, so I called the bar in Divide to see if the river was fishable. There is no better angling barometer than a saloon near the water. Sporting goods stores always say you can catch fish, and they have just the right fly in stock. Resorts and motels have other things to sell. But bars stay busy even when fishing is lousy, and they listen to the stories with a professional ear for bullshit.

The phone rang six times before an out-of-breath barmaid answered. After explaining I lived 150 miles away, I asked about the river.

She laughed. "Oh, it's pitiful, just pitiful. Whole trees are floatin' by. But listen . . . " She turned the phone toward the bar. It sounded like Saturday night, though it was an early Tuesday afternoon. "They can't fish. Business is great." She laughed again. "You comin' down?"

I laughed too. "No, I can do that right here. Thanks."

Too much water muddies the big rivers, but it has to come from somewhere. It comes from little rivers, known colloquially as "cricks." If the Big Hole or the Madison or Rock Creek looks like a chocolate malt, I fish the cricks where cutthroat live, where runoff has already run off.

One is named Bear Creek. I often lie when people ask where I fish, supplying some *nom de stream*, but Bear Creek is this one's real name. And it is full of cutthroat trout. Go ahead. There's no need to thank me.

The canyon itself is narrow, heading on the western side of the continental divide, and the creek is never really muddy, though sometimes it is hard to find, back there in the trees, alders and willows choking the banks. That's why it remains clear, even in late May—it heads in thick timber and runs through thick timber and never leaves thick timber until it flows into suburbia. The snow under the trees melts slowly, shaded by fir and pine and the narrow canyon walls, and the loose forest earth—covered by four or five inches of conifer needles—soaks up most of the meltwater. It eases into the ground rather than rushing off the mountain, and comes back up in springs farther down the canyon, feeding the creek in the heat of August.

The highway is the dividing line. Turn left and you enter a maze of circular gravel roads joining a herd of five-acre ranchettes. Turn right and an old logging road takes you up the creek.

It's an old logging road and the branches on the trees along each side thunk dully against the windshield of the pickup, leaving traces of goat's-beard moss on the side-view mirrors. The tall grass and short pines growing on the hump between the two tracks swish against the front bumper. New logging roads are wider than this, with graded bends, to accommodate big trucks, and don't have pines along their middles.

New logging roads lead to clearcuts. Instead, this one leads through timber almost virgin, Douglas fir and ponderosa pine and western larch. Big trees, I think, until driving past a stump cut when the forest was as pure as mountaintop snow, a stump six feet high and four feet thick, notches cut into the grayed mossy sides a step above the ground, where long-dead loggers pounded slabs to stand on while they pulled a six-foot cross-cut saw.

Driving through the shadows, smelling moss and cool, damp earth, these huge pale gray stumps stand among the smaller, live trees like a tyrannosaurus femur eroding from a desert cliff. It is as if a completely different world existed back then, a forest of much larger beings, so long ago that another world has almost covered the old. A ruffed grouse whirs into the trees and I wonder what kind of birds grew back then, before chain saws.

The two-track enters a clearing a mile up from the highway, the creek flowing through a galvanized culvert under the dirt. For forty feet around the culvert the ground is bulldozed flat, the result of installing the culvert two or three years ago. Before that, the road crossed the stream on a gravel bed. At least the dozer created enough space to park off the trail, in case some other time traveler gets lost up here. Sitting on the tailgate, listening to the engine tick as it cools in the morning, I hear a blue grouse hoot farther up the canyon. I look up at the sun once or twice while pulling on the hip boots, since it may be the last time I'll see it for a few hours.

Threading the six-foot rod is easy. Without a vest or net to tangle in the alders, I start upstream, entering the shadows on foot. The creek disappears quickly in the alders, and I only hear it, walking along the alder edge in damp larch needles, a very different sound than its water made back in the clearing. There it riffled over gravel, the sound steadier than a murmur, more like a hiss. Here it can barely be heard through the thickets, unless it crosses a deadfall, making like a miniature Niagara.

Sometimes I have to stalk these streams for a hundred yards before finding a place where the alders thin. There's almost never a place to walk up to the stream—and absolutely never a place to backcast, unless you count the culverted clearing where no trout live. Even where the alders thin, you have to worm your way through to the bank. I look for the green places before trying.

The green places remind me of Richard Brautigan's description, in *Trout Fishing In America,* of a creek "like 12,845 telephone booths in a row," except here the phone booths are more spread out, as they'd be along a fast-food strip, one on the corner of a 7–11, the next by a gas station down the block. That is as much open space as you can find back in there. There's still no direct sun, but the alder leaves canopying the stream thin just enough over the pool to let a green light through, visible in the gray timber like a lighted phone booth on a drizzly night.

The first one is back in there fifty feet, just visible through crosshatched alders. So I gird my loins (in this case girding means unrolling my shirtsleeves and buttoning them down) and start in.

That's the reason for the short rod—you hold it in front of you, threading it between alders and willows and aspens like a fencing foil. A longer rod, say around seven and a half feet, would actually be more useful for fishing, but it's hell getting it there.

In ten minutes and three rod-tangles I can see the far edge of the pool and slow down, stepping carefully on the unknown earth far below the waist-high layer of fern and young alders. The routine is to ease the rod forward, watching the tip carefully, plucking leaves and green pliable branches off the strung line (I learned long ago that it is impossible to rig a rod once you're inside these jungles, that it's easier to string the line at the pickup and then worm the whole thing through the brush), then take a half-step forward, watching the pool.

Five more minutes finds me just about there, a six-foot fly rod from the middle of the pool. The water bends away from me after falling over a mossed log and has dug a hole perhaps two feet deep in a three-foot-wide stream. By leaning forward behind an alder I can see the edge of the deepest part of the pool, the green light angling down through the water. The bottom of the pool consists of pale gravel, the size of show-off engagement stones, up near the log, fading to geometrically ridged sand toward the tail, three feet below. The sand appears dim and muddy in the cool green light, and then somewhere far overhead a cloud leaves and the sun burns down through the alder leaves and the sand turns almost tawny, flecks of mica scattered along the ridges. And four of the ridges turn into cutthroat trout.

They hold themselves steadily in the current, a foot below the surface, waiting for something to happen. This is what they do for a living, wait in this green hole in this narrow canyon, staring at the deeper water until something falls over the log. Then they swim up and grab it. If it's edible, they swallow. That's what cutthroat do.

So I give 'em something. Threading the rod through the edge of the willows, I try to make the brown tip look like another willow, moving so slowly my shoulders begin to ache from holding up the three-ounce rod. The trick is to angle the rod upward, high above the stream, so that the four feet of leader and deer-hair fly can fall away from the rod and hang above the water. Then I lower the rod slowly, watching the fly, making adjustments until the fly will land in the right place, the just-moving water below the log.

When it does, the fins flare on all four trout and they tip forward slightly, gills moving faster. Then one of the smaller fish starts upward, swimming casually, no fear, tail sweeping from side to side like a leaf easing down through the air. As it nears the fly the sunlight brings out each black spot along its sides, and then I can see the orange under its jaws, the only hot color in the pool.

And the biggest trout, who obviously finds thinking a bother, finally realizes that the small trout is going to eat that fly. And darts upward so fast that the small trout dives sideways and down, the bigger fish splashing like a quarter being dropped in the pool as it takes the fly.

There's not much finesse to fighting a palm-length trout in a telephone booth. I just haul up on the rod and the trout comes along, wriggling in the air for two feet before falling off the hook back into the pool. And that's the end of that phone booth for a while. The phone could ring and ring and nobody would answer.

So I turn around and thread my way out of the alders and head upstream again, looking for more green places. I find three more in the next two hours, one a narrow space between the alders, leaves sweeping the surface on each side, where a really big trout, perhaps a foot long, grabs the fly quickly and then dives around a willow root, breaking me off. The other is a pool much like the first, except the deep water is along my side of the pool and I have to lower the fly in blind faith. When I finally do, on the fourth or fifth try placing the fly just so on the bubble of upwelling current, a cutthroat suddenly appears in the green space below, angling upward with all the confidence of someone walking toward a taxi as the driver holds the open door. The last hole lies behind a two-foot boulder on my side of the stream, the current around the other side. I drop the fly along the far side of the rock, blindly letting it down to the surface, and hear a splash. When I raise the rod, presto, trout in the air.

On the way back down the creek to the pickup I run into the blue grouse I heard hooting earlier, a male strutting in a small clearing, tail fanned and purple throat sacs distending like bagpipes. He tilts his head up toward me, as if thinking will *always* be a bother to him, knowing he gave a hen-blue-grouse call, and what's this? I walk up slowly but casually and when I'm within three steps he starts to waddle off, turgid with lust. Walking steadily, I reach down for his tail and hold it gently, and he looks back over his shoulder in semi-desire, wishing we were the same species. Perhaps that's what it is. Perhaps I sometimes wish I could be a blue grouse or a cutthroat trout and live up Bear Creek in the spring, beyond the highways and real telephone booths and ranchettes.

Montana ranchettes, in case you have never seen any, have many forms. Frequently they are a flat lot covered by grass, three-foot-high ornamental shrubs, with a two-story, two-bath, two-car garage, too-much-mortgage house stuck in the middle.

But quite often they are five acres of mud surrounding a mobile home. In the front yard will be a muddy four-wheel-drive pickup with a snowmobile or ATV in the back, a big car, and very often a semi or log skidder or other large diesel machine. In back will be a plywood dog house, usually filled with a Doberman, Rottweiler, or pit bull, a stack of hay bales, a pile (not stack) of firewood, and a horse. The horse will often be skinny. There will be no grass. Around the mobile home will be chain-link fence, and on the fence will be a sign saying "Private Property, No Trespassing."

A friend has a private name for this type of private property. When we pass one on the way to some place like Bear Creek he looks out the pickup window and says, "Now there's a little piece of heaven."

Bear Creek comes out of the mountains and flows through twelve little pieces of heaven, which is handy for the owners since they don't need to worry about watering their steeds. It is pretty hard on Bear Creek, though. State regulations prohibit damming or otherwise impeding the progress of a stream without a permit (though once you have a permit they don't prevent you from sucking out almost every pint of water), but they don't say anything about livestock stomping it into oblivion.

No trout live in this section of Bear Creek. In fact, almost nothing lives in this section of Bear Creek, or along its banks, except horses and pit bulls. This may be seen as a small-scale environmental tragedy, but it has its good points.

One is that since nothing lives in lower Bear Creek nobody much bothers upper Bear Creek, the part that flows through thick timber. So nobody much bothers me when I go up there. And no other fish dare swim upstream through the ranchettes to bother its cutthroat trout.

In fact, the lack of protection from livestock-stomping has probably saved many a cutthroat trout. This sounds strange but it is true. Cutthroat trout are very pretty fish, their sides a metallic green-bronze scattered irregularly with black spots, like negative galaxies. Under their lower jaws are two lines of orange almost as bright as a flagman's vest.

They are as dumb as they are pretty, dumb in the fly-fishing sense of "not very careful of what they eat." In its infinite wisdom, evolution made cutthroat trout optimists, always looking up. More than any other trout, they like to eat things floating on the surface of streams. Back when Lewis and Clark came through, this worked out pretty well, since the only other salmonids in Montana's east-slope rivers were Rocky Mountain whitefish and, in the upper reaches of the rivers, arctic grayling. Whitefish like to eat insects off the bottoms of rivers, and while grayling like to feed up top like cutthroat, they were always scarcer, even way back when.

On the west slope grayling are replaced by the char known as the bull trout. In the few streams where bull trout live alone, they feed democratically, both on the bottom and top; but where there are cutthroats, bull trout keep down. As the biologists who studied them put it, "there were almost no surficial life forms found in bull trout samples." This means they looked in bull trout stomachs and found no adult insects, the ones that float. The cutthroat always beat bull trout to the surface, so the bull trout gave up.

They do this anywhere they live. In places where they are still the only trout, the rings of their rising can cover a piece of calm water. I've sat at high noon above a mountain lake and watched big cutthroats swim just under the surface, as crowded as goldfish in a bowl, tipping up every few feet to take hatching midges. I've seen the same thing on the Yellowstone River in the park, with a hundred very clumsy fly anglers slapping the water all around the rising fish. To a bull trout, this would be like forsaking the cheeseburger on the bottom for the celery sticks up top, a poor trade no matter how many celery sticks were involved. To a brown trout, it would be a naked-on-Main-Street nightmare, a feeling of vulnerability too horrible to admit even to a psychoanalyst.

In evolutionary terms, surface feeding made sense. Except for those dippy grayling, no other Rocky Mountain fish ate the stuff floating up there, so cutthroat had it to themselves. Then we came along.

We did several anti-cutthroat things. First we logged off a lot of trees. Cutthroat spawn in the spring, their eggs (like many salmonids) lying in stream gravel until they hatch. The eggs need oxygen, so require lots of space between the gravel for flowing, aerated water to wash over them. If the spaces between the gravel fill up with mud or silt or sand, the eggs die. Mud or silt or sand happen to be what wash into streams when humans indiscriminately cut down trees. Once we cut down the trees more grass grew, so we ran cattle on the grass, beating down the streambanks and eroding more silt into the streams.

Then we dumped other trout into the rivers. Humans are fundamentally unsatisfied with the way evolution does things, perhaps resenting our descent from "monkeys." Like the very wise people who brought kudzu to the South and starlings to New England, we brought brook and rainbow and brown trout to the Rockies. Brook trout not only like to eat stuff on the surface of rivers, but they can successfully spawn on mud. Rainbows are closely related to cutthroats and interbreed with them, the rainbow genes becoming dominant. Brown trout lie on the bottom of streams and wait for dumb little cutthroats to rise to the surface to eat. Then the brown trout eat the cutthroats.

Then we caught the hell out of the cutthroats. When I was growing up in the 1960s, there was a famous place to catch cutthroats in Yellowstone Park called Fishing Bridge. Fishing Bridge crosses the river as it leaves the huge lake that occupies the ancient caldera of the Yellowstone Plateau. (Not only the river and the lake but the race of cutthroats themselves are called Yellowstone.) When spring comes around up there in June and July—the lake's surface lies seven thousand feet above sea level—the cutthroats think of love and start to drift down the river to spawn. From Fishing Bridge you could lean over the water and see hundreds of big trout, and catch hell out of them. Fishing in the park was free. The trout were easily caught. Not many tourists thought of what they would do with a dozen cutthroat trout on a hot day in July. Garbage cans along the bridge often filled with rotting cutthroats. In those days, if you caught a fish you killed it.

Those things happen most in low places, river valleys and creek bottoms. That's where silt from logging clearcuts builds in stream gravel, and where other trout were dumped in rivers.

And most people fish along roads, and most mountain roads follow rivers and streams.

So most cutthroat trout live in higher places, where people haven't had as many chances to finagle nature. A botany professor of mine noted that scientists come from all over the world to study Rocky Mountain rivers, because the "natural systems" of the West haven't been too terribly disfigured. This becomes truer the higher you climb, up side canyons to glacial lakes. There are few rivers left where cutthroat are the dominant trout, and very few flow in big valleys. The two that come to mind, the upper reaches of the Snake and the Yellowstone, head along the continental divide in the highest valleys where big rivers can live.

Some other cutthroat streams, the creeks that flow into the big rivers, are oddly protected by what might be called "bovine blockading." This happens when the ranchland along a river valley is overgrazed. When a lot of cows live in one place the vegetation grows shorter. Some gets eaten, some gets squashed where they bed down, and some gets stomped. If the cattle live there long enough a cool five-foot-wide willow-bordered creek full of deep pools turns into a warm shallow ten-foot-wide riffle with bare banks. Not many fish live in it, certainly none over a few inches long.

This is not always caused by bovines. Crowd a bunch of little pieces of heaven together, as along Bear Creek, and the same thing can happen. But it happens most often when ranchers, those stewards of the land, run too many cows too long in one place. Ranchers doing this are not unusual.

Environmentalists call this creek-stomping "riparian degradation," and fight for laws to stop it. This is mostly a good thing, but it might be bad for some cutthroat creeks, because without stomped lowland, the high cutthroat creeks would have been invaded by other trout long ago.

I've seen this along most river valleys. The larger tributaries, whose lower reaches have enough flow to stay alive even when stomped, get invaded by alien trout from the big rivers, usually brook trout but often rainbows. Only the smaller creeks are cut off, isolating the cutthroat upstream. To preserve the pure cutthroat in any of its subspecies, it might help to let the stomping go along those creeks.

River grayling have some of the same problems, except worse. They are salmonids, but somewhat distant from the trouts, salmons, and chars—delicate fish that in Montana streams hardly ever weigh more than a pound. Some people call them freshwater sailfish because grayling wear a dorsal fin as egregious as Dolly Parton's breasts. But except for that fin, they're subtle compositions—streamlined silver fish washed with almost subliminal purples and golds. The overall effect is not unlike 1961 Cadillac tailfins welded to a Rolls Royce.

Originally found all through the Missouri River upstream from the Great Falls, grayling now live only in the upper Big Hole and Madison. This last recently startled the Montana Department of Fish, Wildlife and Parks, who thought grayling had disappeared from the Madison drainage except in a lake or two. Some anglers could have told them differently a long time ago but didn't, perhaps because they feared FWP might "help" Madison grayling just as it "helped" cutthroat for so many years: by treating them like any other trout. Now FWP thinks there may be a thousand grayling left in the Madison and another three thousand in the Big Hole. Now you cannot keep them anymore, and FWP is "urging" anglers to release cut-throat as well.

Like Woody Allen, the grayling's problems rise from over-sensitivity to almost anything. For the most part they're a sub-arctic fish, common around the earth in cold pure streams. In Alaska they're ubiquitous as mosquitoes. Some biologists now guess that grayling move downstream during winter, into the lower, warmer pools of bigger rivers, when the icy upper tribu-taries freeze. This may be partly why they've almost disap-peared in Montana: their winter hotels are full of brown and rainbow and brook trout. A grayling wintering in the lower Jefferson would be like moving Jackie Onassis to the Steel Belt. She knows the right moves among the champagne-and-yacht crowd, but is a little too lofty for shots-and-beers and unem-ployment checks.

It may be that our systems aren't so natural, and getting less so. That since this is the most southern place grayling could ever tolerate (along with upper Michigan, a system that turned unnatural a few decades back) the fish is doomed, at least in the rivers of the lower 48.

Grayling don't get much support from nonresident anglers, either. Connecticut yuppies and California silicon commuters tend to fish the famous rivers during the famous hatches, for brown and rainbow trout, because that's where status lies. You cannot blame them. I grew up here and to me the Madison was just the river we drove alongside when we went down to see Old Faithful. In my childhood mind, river and geyser held equal status with the local trout hatchery. It wasn't until after growing a little older and living in the Midwest for a while that I realized that most people didn't get to see Old Faithful each July, or have moose clatter down Main Street in the winter, or catch brown trout from the Madison River any weekend of the summer.

It affected me too, after I'd lived in other places. The first time I came back on a visit and fished the Madison I almost hyperventilated, full of windy tales of hallowed water. Then I moved back and found that the Madison is a good trout stream, but no better than many others. And it didn't have many grayling and cutthroat.

By then I'd become enamored with natural systems. Some of it came from living in the Corn Belt, where nature came in long tall rows. Even walking in the country you were never out of sight of a farmhouse, though admittedly some were abandoned. The best fishing was below a big dam, a park where everybody picnicked and the local walleye whiz could catch fish while people watched.

A woman I worked with thought this was wilderness. She'd moved from Washington, D.C., and from that perspective it was. To me it was claustrophobic. I talked so much about mountains that another coworker allowed as how they were pretty to drive through but made TV reception lousy.

After returning I could see the valley rivers more clearly. They were damn good brown trout rivers, but as natural systems they lacked something. Comparing a river full of European trout and bordered by irrigated hay fields to a grayling-and-cutthroat river was like comparing a hillside full of fenced Herefords to the buffalo plains. A cattle ranch looks wild to someone from Baltimore, but not to someone who grew up reading Lewis and Clark. I fished the Madison and Gallatin and Big Hole, but my eyes often wandered upward, above the hay fields.

Systems become more natural just above the cow-stomped

valleys, along streams like Bear Creek, but they really grow
wild where summers are too short for people. The higher you
climb, the more water, some in solid form even in July. After
the cutthroat creeks of late May, I liked to follow spring uphill,
where opposing seasons sometimes meet head-on.

The first was a creek draining into the Gallatin Valley. Down
there, it grew big enough to withstand the valley cattle. Between the barbed wire and cottonwoods there were deep slow
holes where rainbow and brook trout lived, and even a few
browns up from the big river.

But in the mountains the creek lived in a steep canyon. Its
pools rose like stairsteps made of large rocks, and the water fell
down the mountain so fast that nothing clung to the upper
rocks, not algae or insects, so standing in the middle of the
white water wasn't as bad as it looked: Despite the hard current, felt soles stuck to the rocks like a packhorse's steel shoes,
and you could stand braced against cataracts, the skin of your
thighs buzzing from the irrhythmic push of heavy water. As
long as those thighs could take it, you could stand on the rocks
of one pool and look at eye level along the surface of the next.
Sometimes during a hot July day, when small mayflies hatched,
you looked along the soft airy roil of the water of the pool above
and saw the dark heads of trout as they came up, like black
bubbles rising in white air.

There were rainbow in the canyon, but farther up, beyond
several small falls, there were only cutthroat. The trout hid in
the bottom of the pools and only came up for a sure thing. So
you tried to lay the line over a rock in the pool, draping it above
the current, so the fly (made of hollow deer hair and greased
like a bodybuilder) could dance around on the rising bubbles

until the trout were convinced they could nail it from any angle. Eventually one would.

Even then I wanted to climb higher. The stream headed in a series of cirques, circular valleys carved by glaciers, that stairstepped up to the top of the mountains like the pools of the stream below. You could drive to the first, lowest cirque on a gravel road, but it held only a willow swamp full of moose and, during the brief summer, mosquitoes. But from the end of the road a path followed the higher ground through fir and spruce around the swamp to the higher cirques.

The first time we hiked it was in late July, I and a young woman I was in love with, and a friend with whom I'd worked on a cattle ranch in eastern Montana. This was long before any of us could afford aluminum-framed packs and light tents and sleeping bags, so we loaded up some army rucksacks with sandwiches and orange juice and started out early, before the sun came over the divide above us. We saw one moose a quarter-mile away, a cow that probably had a calf hidden in the willows.

The path left the timber above the willow swamp and followed the creek, rising more steeply. Soon we found snowbanks in the shade among the boulders, and once we crossed a snowbank that bridged the stream, our footprints pink in the white snow. A long time later I learned this was caused by an algae that blooms in midsummer up there. In some places flowers grew through the snow. Then I couldn't name then; now I probably could, but it didn't make any difference then, and doesn't now.

The trail grew steeper and began switching back and forth as it worked its way up the moraine of the lake above. This is typical of mountain lakes: The glacier that formed the cirque pushed gravel and boulders and earth ahead of it, leaving a natural dam at the mouth of the valley when it receded. So the trail grows steepest just below the lake, when you are very tired. This makes you feel you deserve everything you find, flowers or snow bridges or large cutthroat trout.

Toward the top of the moraine the boulders and snow thinned and the earth leveled out into a lawn as even and green as a golf course, surrounded by a distant half-circle of straight cliffs taller than most skyscrapers. Along the bases of the cliffs lay boulder fields that looked like gravel from our distance. As we walked along the fairway more flowers appeared, yellow and purple and blue, and then the lake. The lawn ran up to its edge, as level and clean as a Japanese garden, and as we walked up I half-expected to see goldfish.

Instead there were cutthroat trout, swimming just under the surface and tipping up calmly like goldfish after invisible in-sects. None of them were longer than the span of my hand from thumb to pinky tip, but in the absolute clarity of the water they looked more attainable than any wild fish we'd ever seen, as if the precision of seeing made them more real.

We had two rods among the three of us, a spinning rod belonging to my cowboy friend, and my cheap fly rod. The cowboy had a few nightcrawlers and hooks, and two spinners. I had just started tying flies and had some small green Woolly Worms, the only true pattern I was capable of, and a few hunks of deer hair wound on hooks, a fly of my own design. Or perhaps more correctly, a fly of my own accident.

The cowboy cast a worm out that scared several cutthroats as it landed. We watched the worm sink to the bottom, and then waited. Soon the little trout started feeding again, on whatever invisible item they found on the surface, while the worm lay very visibly on the bottom of the lake. The cowboy got tired of this and tied on a spinner. This scared even more trout. It was up to me.

I tied on one of the deer-hair accidents and cast as hard as I could. This meant that one out of three casts dropped behind and caught wildflowers. But eventually one cast landed fifteen or twenty feet out in the lake and I had sense enough to let the fly sit there. Soon a cutthroat trout came by, tipped up, and ate it. I yanked on the line and the trout flew through the air, landing in the flowers behind me.

We kept moving around the edge of the lake, toward the upper end, where we'd heard a creek entered. An older angler had told us that creek mouths were always good places to fish in lakes, and as we looked for the creek we kept fishing, trading the fly rod back and forth. Sometimes the cowboy tried his spinner again and scared more fish. My technique did not catch any more fish, but then neither did anybody else's.

By the time we worked around to the upper end of the lake the sun was almost straight overhead. This was the first time any of us had felt the sun through the thin air on top of the world, and despite the cool air, the light felt heavier. The creek came into the lake in the shadow of a steep timbered slope. The shadow felt cool, and out where the creek's current faded into the lake, we could see the curve of rising fish touching the surface without waves, as if the stream had decided on a last finishing kick before going gently into that good night.

The fish were rising out beyond our casting range, but I tried anyway, the line collapsing in coils on the stream's current. I said something, frustrated, and was about to try again when my woman friend noticed the line uncoiling, pulled out into the lake, and told me to chrissake leave it on the water. Soon it uncoiled and floated in an almost straight undulant line, and in a few second I felt a pluck at the fly. I lifted the rod and a fish jumped out there, on the edge of the current. Then it stayed under the water, turning hard against the rod. When I stripped it in we could see the high curve of a grayling's dorsal, the fish wriggling sideways, tipped toward the bottom of the lake. When I dragged it out of the water onto the green grass it felt as if I'd caught a caribou, or perhaps even a very tiny mammoth.

I tried the same cast again and it worked. The second grayling jumped more than the first, and was slightly bigger. Then I caught a cutthroat. The cowboy asked for one of my deer-hair accidents and tied it on his spinning line, clamped a split shot to the line, then held the rod's tip in the creek mouth and let the line wash out into the lake. Soon he had a grayling too. Then the woman I loved took the fly rod and, while I cleaned the small collection of fish, caught several more. We took turns with the two rods, catching fish on every "cast," and took turns cleaning them and packing them in a small snowbank at the base of the mountainside behind us.

Soon we had caught almost all the fish we could legally keep and still we kept catching them, releasing the rest, looking for one or two big ones. I had caught perhaps fifty when the rod bent over hard and the wet fly line slipped through my hands for a foot or so before I caught it again. The fish rolled once on the surface, as if to show me its size, and the cowboy shouted. By then I had sense enough to just hold the rod up and let the fish tire, and after a long time, too long without seeing the fish again, it came close to the bank and the cowboy lay down in the grass and scooped it with his whole arm up onto shore, a cut-throat trout two-thirds as long as his arm, with a belly like a horse that's fed on meadow grass all summer. I dropped the rod and grabbed the fish as it flopped along the shore, a cutthroat trout so full of eggs that when I picked it up a thin translucent line of orange pushed out of its belly like a leak from a water balloon. And then I knew what the hard stomachs of the few small cutthroat I'd cleaned were full of—eggs from bigger fish that were spawning at the mouth of the creek, here in mid-July, springtime in the high Rockies.

We killed the big fish and cleaned it carefully, the cowboy saying the eggs were good to eat, too. We lay the fish and its eggs in the snowbank next to the smaller fish and tried to catch some more, but the cheap thrill of catching fish on every cast had left and the shadow reached halfway across the lake. The gray limestone cliffs beyond had started turning yellow with the angled sun, and we packed the fish in a plastic bag with hard crystallized snow to keep them cold and headed back down the mountain, not seeing any moose along the way. We went back to the small old apartment where the woman and I lived and she fried up grayling and cutthroat and cutthroat eggs and we washed them down with cheap beer. The cowboy got very drunk and passed out on our couch. Sometime in the night the woman and I made love. Two years later the cowboy, drunk again, smashed his pickup head-on into a car on some late-night highway and ended up paralyzed, and a few years later the woman and I fell out of love.

But that is what grayling are for: to live in places so pure that people cannot live there, where fish must eat everything put in front of them to survive, with the sort of uncompromising innocence that lets us believe we can drive drunk at ninety miles an hour through the dark, or that all love lasts forever and ever, or we can catch fish any time we want. Sometimes that is more valuable than all the brown trout in the Madison, or all the unnatural systems of our world.

A Trout Stream Named Desire

> Too much of a good thing can be wonderful.
> — MAE WEST

Most western Native American tribes had a saying about grizzly tracks—about fishing or hunting someplace else when you found them. A few weeks ago I came around a bend on a mountain trail in the Bob Marshall Wilderness and found myself within sixty feet of a boar grizzly. I didn't recall any Indian sayings at the time, but the idea of fishing someplace else suddenly made a lot of sense.

This was a big bear. The fact that he was eating grass was not comforting, because I was close enough to hear the roots tear-

ing. I whispered to my companion, close behind me, something like, "There's a goddamn grizzly." Perhaps the adjective
was more vehement. The bear looked up and we backed around
the bend, quickly and quite a ways. We weren't sure the bear
knew what we were, so we decided to talk loudly, to let him
know people were around. Bears are truly wild in the Bob—not
like Glacier Park's bears, who sometimes charge tourists to
make them drop their daypacks full of granola bars.

So we talked loudly and soon heard something large moving
off through the alders above the trail. When we peeked around
the bend again the bear was gone.

That encounter had three effects. The first was fright. After
calming down, this seemed healthy, a sort of atavistic computer
check of all my systems. If a large grizzly bear alarms me, I
figure my nerves are still approximately as they evolved, not
too warped by civilization.

After fright came a thrill. An innocent bystander might sug-
gest that the same thrill could be had by climbing a vertical
rock face. No. Unlike rock climbing, or whitewater rafting, or
bungee jumping, or any of the dangerous pursuits some of us
use to persuade ourselves that there is indeed life in the twen-
tieth century, grizzlies do not thrill us when and where we
choose. You do not choose to climb a grizzly—through he may
choose to climb you. Living (if only for a few days) in grizzly
country is like a tune-up after the computer check: It makes
sure everything keeps turning over. Even in the moment before falling asleep, you are extremely sure you're alive.

But the third response was unexpected: a moment of recognition. Anyone who spends time around bears gains some of
that; bears are sometimes too human. One reason people and

bears have problems is that we like the same summer places: lakes, creek bottoms, berry patches, high cool mountains. Anyone who's had a black bear stand up a few yards away in a huckleberry meadow experiences a certain recognition, something like surprising Uncle Bill unbuttoning his overalls out in the weeds at the family picnic, if a trifle more startling.

But the face on that grizzly was unlike any black bear's. Black bears often look slightly unfocused, like Uncle Bill after his fifth beer, their long sloping faces seeming in need of a pair of reading glasses. But this grizzly was grizzly in the extreme: a chocolate bear with gray-blond trim, head as big as a beach ball, and when he lifted that head his wide-set eyes looked straight forward from a flat face, unmoving and totally focused. It was odd, but it was as if I saw a cautious knowledge there—a knowledge of being separate yet equal, the only two animals every other animal is afraid of. This didn't mean I wanted to hug the grizzly, like an old friend. But suddenly I recognized the terror that other animals feel for us, the terror they find in our flat faces and totally focused eyes—and even more than giving me empathy for a deer or trout, it gave me empathy for the bear. Being a grizzly must be a damn lonely profession, perhaps as lonely as being human.

Anyone who watches bears sees them looking for really good stuff to eat, scratching their backs, being startled by things as small as squirrels. But most of all you notice how they want to be alone. With the exceptions of lovers and immediate family, bears are strict individualists. Even when gathered on salmon streams, they observe codes of avoidance, small bears keeping out of the way of big bears, and especially not looking directly into larger bears' eyes. Up in the mountains, away from the enforced closeness of salmon, small black bears run when big black bears show up—and big black bears run like hell when grizzlies come round.

We are more like bears than we like to admit. Left to our natural devices in emptier country, we tend to spread out. We act like bears, good for occasional society but for the most part happier when alone or with one or two good friends.

Even when driving, the pattern is there. In the West there are always a few tailgaters, but all they want to do is pass, to get to the next town or next bar. But in much of this nation there are too many of us—we are the most numerous mammal on earth—and most of us live in crowds. We've become conditioned to crowding. Driving the back roads of Florida, I've run into retiree convoys, lines of maybe half a dozen cars with New York plates, zooming bumper to bumper along an empty highway between sand pines and palmettoes. Are these people related? Are they traveling together for protection, like a wagon train? No, they grew up driving bumper to bumper on the highways of Westchester County and Long Island and feel uncomfortable with any space between them and the next car.

Like bears, anglers tend to gather at the good fishing places, like the Henry's Fork and Madison and Big Horn. But as those places have grown more crowded I've noticed fewer local license plates. Perhaps it's the instinct of a bear who grew up unconditioned to crowds, but it always seemed that trout fishing should be a lonely occupation. Of course, the loneliest anglers I've ever seen were fishing a stream in Connecticut, not far from the New York line. We were taking the train from Danbury to meet a relative who'd drive us to Shea Stadium, where the Mets would play the Pirates, and for a while the tracks were parallel to a small creek. On the other side of the creek were a broad lawn and then some office buildings, and at each small pool of the creek was a fly fisherman (there were no women), plying his lonely craft on that pool and that pool only, looking as happy as a banker at a board meeting.

But the lonely I'm talking about is a different sort, a lonely freedom. Like grizzly bears, we should be able to fish where we want to, the reason the famous places have not really appealed to me. Lately there's been lots of press about how crowded even the Henry's Fork and Big Horn are getting. Well, they are, if not quite as crowded as the creeks between Danbury and Shea Stadium. But there are hundreds of trout streams out there—in the big Out There, the Rocky Mountain West— where a wader track is about as common as a grizzly's. After a time along such streams, the print of a felt-soled boot begins to look remarkably like the broad track of a bear, even without claw marks. Like any good hunter-gatherer, I have developed an aversion to each.

These are not mountain streams, either, but meadow streams, ranch streams, valley streams that flow between cottonwood groves and alfalfa fields and Hereford pastures. They are not strictly natural systems—for the most part they hold brown and rainbow and brook trout—but they are places where you can fish alone, for stream-bred trout. They do take time to find, something we seem to have a shortage of these days. Time is money, and trout are not money. You can buy them or earn them, but not spend them.

Like Ulysses and his oar, I earn these trout by wandering back into the hills and valleys until I find a place where, when I knock on a ranch-house door and ask permission to fish, the gentle folk within are startled, as if one of their Herefords just asked for a steak dinner. Where it is beyond anyone's comprehension why some fool would bother to ask to catch a trout. Like being a grizzly bear, it is a lonely life, but someone has to live it.

Streams usually cut a deep hole just below bridges. Abutments are spaced to accommodate normal water levels; during floods the widened current accelerates through the gap and carves away at the streambed. The hole on the downstream side of this one-lane wooden bridge, even in low August water, was "deep enough to float your hat," as an alcoholic ranch hand I worked with used to say. There was no railing and I leaned out the open window of the pickup and looked directly down into the deep water, thanking God it was not gin clear.

The pool was a translucent green, the color of a trillion phytoplankton yearning to breathe free. I reached into the ashtray for a new penny and dropped it into the pool, risking arrest for heavy-metals pollution. It disappeared a couple of feet below the surface. As it disappeared a fish tried for it, a green-silver curve deep in the water.

"How's it look?" Eileen asked, from the other side of the cab.

I turned and looked past her, upstream, where the shadows of cottonwood trees leaned across the water. The evening light between our bridge and the cottonwoods was filled with caddisflies, appearing white as they flew through the sun against the shadows, vibrating like a quick galaxy. "It looks good," I said. A blue heron took off, unfolding out of the shadows and heading upstream, made nervous by our stopping. Eileen pointed. "Too bad he left," I said. "I was going to ask how the fishing was."

The home place was a half-mile back, a two-story white frame house at the end of a gravel road bordered by more cottonwoods. The rancher had just sat down to eat, he said, otherwise he would have shown us where to fish, a half-mile downstream. "It's too thick by the bridge," he explained. "Lots of trees and willows. Not many folks fish there."

"That's okay," I said. "We'll take our chances." We thanked him, and he said if we were to come by again, just go ahead and fish, don't even ask. He'd know our outfit.

There was a place to pull off just on the other side of the bridge, a barbwire gate leading into a hay field. We sat on the tailgate and pulled on hip boots, then walked along the edge of the field to the cottonwoods, Eileen carrying the rod. Near the trees a whitetail buck jumped up from the tall grass, summer antlers full grown and thickened with velvet, as brick red as the rest of his body, and stood for one terrorized instant before running upstream through the trees, high tail visible like a firefly even after his body disappeared in shadow. We stood and watched, two clawless bears, then walked through low rose bushes under the trees to the edge of the stream. Both upstream and down from the cottonwoods we could see willows lining the bank, but the tall trees shaded out everything underneath them except the roses. Everywhere was the taste of late summer, heat and dust and the sweet-raw taste of willows and hay in our mouths.

A gravel bar angled across from the far shore, curving into the bank below us. On the far side the water looked deeper, and as we stood and looked I saw a trout rise in the bubbles below the bar.

"There's your trout," I said. That summer she had decided to learn to fly fish, as the water dropped and I started catching more trout on dry flies than she did on spinners. I pointed with my rod. "Over there, in the deep water."

She shaded her eyes and looked. "I can't see it."

"It looks like the bubbles, except slower." I watched and saw the same trout come up, and then another, farther downstream. "There's one below him now, in the slick water."

"I see that one. Are they eating those flies?" She pointed at the caddis in the air.

I shook my head. "They're rising too slow. Those are all in the air, anyway, not the water." I watched the trout rise again. "They probably eat anything that comes floating along." I squatted down and sat back on the edge of the bank, then eased my legs into the river, onto the firm gravel. Suddenly my feet felt pleasantly cool, and the shadows seemed cooler too, as if the riverbed held two rivers, one of water and one of cool air flowing just above the water. I turned and held her hand as she eased into the water, then started across, angling up the gravel bar, the water less than shin-deep. In the middle of the river I looked upstream. The water quickened again above the pool in front of us, but beyond I could see the current slowing into another pool.

We shuffled our feet slowly under the surface, moving within a short cast of where the lower trout rose. She whispered, as if we were stalking the whitetail buck, "Is the fly on my line okay?"

"You don't have to whisper," I said. "Just don't splash." She looked at me, frowning. She likes to get close to anything wild. She likes to fool all their senses, and was extremely disappointed to find wild turkeys can't smell. "Let me see it," I said. It was a small, sparse Elkhair Caddis that had been on the leader for a week now, since I'd last used the rod. I took a plastic container of line grease from my vest pocket and worked a little into the hair and hackle. It was an old fly, made before I started crushing every barb in the vise before I tied the fly, so I flattened the barb with the needle-nose pliers from my vest. "Okay," I said, letting the fly go. "Catch him."

She pulled some line from the reel and began false-casting, a little too fast.

"Wait on the backcast," I said. We'd gone through this all week, on the lawn.

She nodded, and did better. When she had enough line out she cast, the line landing in a snaking curve four feet below the fish. Her lips tightened and she breathed hard through her nose.

"That's okay," I said. "It's better if it isn't straight. Just let out a little more line and do the same thing again."

So she did, dropping two coils of line right on top of the trout's last rise.

"That's a little too much," I said. "He won't come up for a while now."

She shook her head, stripping in line. The coils caught one another and the line came up in a tangle. I held the rod while she picked at it. "You warned me," she said.

"About what?"

"About having to learn a whole new set of tangles."

"You remember. You always say there are too many things to remember."

"This is real—" She held up the tangled line. "None of that 'accelerate the cast' stuff." She smiled, looking up, the line finally untangled. "Now what?"

"The other's still rising, up in the bubbles."

She looked, bent forward like a heron. "Now I see him. When he comes up, it's like a longer, slower bubble."

I nodded. "Try to put it in the fast water at the edge of the rocks. Then let it float into the bubbles. He'll find it."

She nodded, very serious, and bent forward again when she let the line go. The fly landed perfectly at the base of the gravel bar. I lost it in the shadows but watched the yellow line. The trout curved up in the bubbles beyond the tip.

"He just took it."

She shook her head.

"Yes, he did. I saw him, right beyond your line."

"Then he didn't eat the fly. I never felt a thing."

"You don't feel them. You watch, then raise the rod."

"You never told me that part!"

"Well, it's obvious. Look at the slack in the line. You have to raise the rod to hook the fish."

"I never had to before."

"With lures you always have a tight line. With flies, you have to strike as soon as they take the fly. Otherwise they let it go."

"You mean they spit it out."

I winced. "You've seen a trout's mouth. They don't have spitting gear."

"That's not what Milo told me, that time we went fishing up Rock Creek. He said the trout spit my lure out."

"It's just something people say. Besides, you know Milo."

"Yes, and you know everything, but you don't tell me to raise the rod when the fish eats my fly."

I rolled my eyes. "Okay, okay. I thought you'd watched me enough to know."

She didn't say anything, just started casting again. She false-cast for a while, drying the fly, remembering that, and then let the line go. The sun had moved over the head of the pool, and I could see the fly floating between the bubbles, looking very phony. And then the trout took it, coming up in a curve so slow I could see his dorsal. "He—" I started to say, but the trout was already in the air.

"I got him!" she shouted. The trout jumped again, downstream, a rainbow bigger than I expected.

"Yes, you did."

She laughed. "What do I do?"

"The same thing you do with a lure. Let him go until he's tired. Let him have a little line if you think he's pulling too hard."

He jumped three more times, twice in the downstream shadows, then the last time upstream in the sunlight, so bright he almost hurt my eyes. After that he stayed underwater. She kept the rod up and when the trout began to tire I unhooked the net from the back of my vest and knelt down, feeling gravel and cool water under my knee, through the waders. "Back up and lead him over it," I said.

She held the rod up with both hands and waded backward, standing behind me, and the trout came up and slid over the black water and then over the aluminum rim. When I lifted the net he felt too heavy, like an aspirin bottle full of lead shot. I reached down and twisted the tiny fly out of his mouth, then held the net in the water, letting him breathe.

She squatted beside me, very elegant in jeans and hip boots, and looked at her trout. He had an olive back and a pale wash of pink over his gill covers and flanks, as if someone had painted a new chrome bumper with diluted nail polish. She shook her head. "Let me let him go," she said. I handed her the net. "He's heavy," she said, looking at me. I nodded. Then she tipped the net up and he went.

We straightened and looked upstream, at the bottom of the next pool. "Your turn," she said, and handed me the rod. I looked at her. "Thanks," she said. "Sorry I got mad."

I shrugged. "I've done it so long, I forget what I have to tell you."

She nodded. We walked up the gravel bar to the bottom of the next pool. The cottonwoods ended and there was a long stretch of undercut grassy bank above deep water. We stood and watched, but no trout came up.

"There has to be one in there," she said, whispering again.

I nodded. "Probably, if there are rainbows like you caught so close to the road." I took a small box from one of the bottom pockets of my vest and found a deer-hair grasshopper. I bit off the light tippet and tied the hopper onto the heavier leader, curling up the tippet and Elkhair Caddis and putting them in the box. Then I greased the hopper up like an English Channel swimmer.

The undercut was all in shadow and I first cast down at the tail, in six inches of water. At dusk you never know. Nothing happened, so I took a step upstream and cast again. By the time we'd reached the middle of the cut bank I had the range just right and was tossing the hopper into the loose overhanging grass about half the time, pulling it out to drop along the edge of the bank.

Then the water bulged up under the fly like the surface of a Florida pond when a sunken alligator decides to leave, and I jerked my rod hand slightly, involuntarily, and then stopped it voluntarily, because I could still see the fly. The slight jerk pulled the fly toward us, sinking it. Then it bobbed up again, and the trout hit it, head coming out of the water like a small gator. The rod was already halfway up from my involuntary jerk and the fish hooked itself when it turned back toward the cut bank, water flying. I leaned the rod sideways, trying to keep the fish out of the shadows, and the trout rolled on the surface.

"Brown," somebody said, and I realized it was me.

"Catch him," Eileen said. "Catch that sonofabitch." She gets like that, the city Irish kid who finally learned to fish. She would have been a good poacher, back in County Mayo, having that hard need to possess wild things, no matter what the cost.

The heavy tippet held and the trout held in the deeper water below the bank, bending the rod rhythmically in the slow cadence of a bass drum. I'd seen other big brown trout fighting the hook and could imagine his length bending, like a muscular hinge, as he tossed his head.

When that didn't do him any good he turned and headed downstream, through the shallow riffle, sucking the slack line through my fingers until it all disappeared and the reel whirred. I stuck my left hand inside the reel and touched the hard-wound line to slow the spool. He made it over the lip of the bar and I followed, walking fast through the shallow water, not caring if I splashed now, feeling the trout tossing his head again as I wound line back onto the reel. I held the rod high, standing above him at the edge of the pool, feeling sweat on my forehead, suddenly cool in the evening. Then he stopped bending, holding steady in the stream. When I leaned back he came toward me, then ran across-stream, still strong but not uncontrollable, and I knew I had him.

Eileen knew it too. "Let me take the net," she said, standing behind me.

"I don't know if he'll fit." I pumped the rod now, dropping it as I reeled, then lifting again, and he came halfway across the pool, then ran again, not as strong.

She took the net anyway, unhooking it from my back, and by then I could see him, turning in the dark water. He was lean, not belly-heavy like the rainbow, lower jaw hooked like an osprey's. When I leaned back to try to move him toward the net he came and then turned again. Then I said the hell with it, I'd either break him off or land him, and brought him up and over the net, at the edge of the bar, and Eileen lifted.

His head hung just under the aluminum frame, but his tail stuck up above the other side. He was the color of the gravel under our feet, an old bronze, with red spots broken up by his scales. I breathed out and thought about killing him. He'd taste fine, cut into steaks and broiled with some butter and garlic and basil. Then I twisted the grasshopper out of the bone of his jaw and said, "Let's get him in the water."

We both knelt again, in the same place we'd knelt to release Eileen's trout. She dipped the net and I held the trout, both my hands under his lean belly, weightless in the current. His gill covers worked and he breathed among the bubbles.

"There's lots of air in that water," I said. Eileen nodded. "Sometimes I wonder," I said, holding the trout.

"Wonder about what?"

"Wonder about making trout swim up and down streams until they almost kill themselves."

She nodded again.

The trout moved in my hands. I took my upstream hand

away, holding him gently by the wrist of his tail. Then he swam away, bending in a slow cadence, the same color as the new penny I dropped over the edge of the bridge.

"Next time, trout," I said. "Next time, I'll eat you."

A few years and three months later a high pressure system moved up from Utah. November fishing is like spring: better after two or three days of sun, in the afternoons when the chill is off the water. So we waited one day, worked the next morning, then headed for the bridge after lunch.

The leaves had been on the ground for three weeks now, all the grass and brush and trees along the river various shades of brown, from the bright tan crested wheatgrass to the rough gray-brown bark of cottonwoods to the smooth red-brown of peach-leaf willow. Even the wheat stubble had lost its metallic sheen. We didn't expect to jump a whitetail buck; by this time they'd be hiding back in the willow thickets, sensitive velvet stripped from their antlers.

But we did find tracks along the stubble edge, and fresh rubs on two alders when we entered the brush, the bark stripped away at thigh level. Looking closer, there were deep furrows in the green wood from a buck's antler tines. Farther on we found a piece of ground, as big around as a small coffee table, scraped bare under a hanging branch, with one clear hoofprint in the damp dark earth and a faint musk on the air. I pointed to the bare earth. Eileen nodded. The rut had begun, and a buck was baiting his rub-line like a trapper after mink.

Spring is thought of as the time of love, but that is mostly because of birds and bees, rather scatterbrained beings willing to make love in public. Many wild things replicate in fall, usually in secret places: whitetails in willow thickets, bighorn sheep in mountain cirques, and brown trout in the gravel of cold streams.

I used to write down dates of various wild matings I observed, but after a while learned that numbers don't make the best calendars. True, most temperate-zone animals mate at certain times of year, so their young (fawns, chicks, troutlings) will be born during a good period for survival. These deer, for instance, would mate over the next two to three weeks, across the middle of November, fawns gestating over about two hundred days to be born within the two or three weeks around June first, with the first summer burst of high-protein green. Similarly, brown trout would spawn now, eggs hatching in the first warming water of spring, insect life skittering over the creek-bottom gravel to gobble the first algae. Oh, how wise is Nature.

But how do they know? Most mating occurs when days are a certain length—what biologists call *photoperiod*. As the days shorten in fall, female brown trout grow orange eggs in their bellies, and male white-tailed deer rub the bark from alders with their antlers. Everything gets ready—and then *boom*, a year of lust gets packed into three weeks.

But the boom doesn't occur just because a certain day had nine hours and thirty-three minutes between sunrise and sunset. As a fisheries biologist friend put it, "Photoperiod is the dynamite, temperature is the blasting cap." The right temperature sets them off, trout and deer and birds and bees. No candlelight, no wine, no dancing. Just light and heat, or the lack thereof.

Eventually, I found my calendars nothing more than notes. It takes a few years to get the feel of light and heat, the peculiar combinations that bring the boom. Wild Merriam's turkeys usually begin gobbling in the hills beyond the river in mid-April, but if a late snowstorm comes down from Alberta they'll stop as if slapped. If the cold hangs around a few days, they'll huddle in the branches of ponderosa pines and say nothing, soaking up light and very little heat. But the first sunny day, with pasque flowers blooming along the edges of melting snow? Boom.

It becomes a combination of feel and observation, some of it direct: When whitetail bucks' necks swell, something is about to happen. But brown trout, I have found, don't begin spawning until the leaves fall from the cottonwoods. That could happen as early as mid-October in a cold year, or as late as the last week of the month in a warm one. (In the East there's the shadbush, a variety of the bush westerners call Juneberry or serviceberry, and Canadians call Saskatoons, that blooms when the shad run upstream to spawn. We once parked our pickup camper along the Delaware River around the first of May, and were eating our evening meal, after dark, when someone pounded hard on the door. "Are they here yet?" It was a young man who wanted to know if the shad were running. He'd seen a camper with a canoe on top and knew we had to be after shad; in the dark he couldn't see the Montana plates. In the morning I got up and stepped outside to see serviceberries—shadbushes—blooming on the hills above the river.)

It works in quirky ways. In early fall, the days shorter, male turkeys start to crank up their gobbles again, usually right after the equinox. The photoperiod isn't right—the day-length equivalent of late April would be late August—but it isn't until late September that the days are cool enough to delude them into thinking it's spring. About the same time a few male sharp-tailed grouse "dance" on flat-topped ridges, and ruffed grouse drum in the foothill aspens. They are all, of course, doomed to disappointment, because no matter what their light/heat clocks say, Nature won't let the females go along with off-season foolishness. (At least most of the time. Biologists have found newborn mule deer in every month of the year in Montana; Nature is not written in stone, and there has to be variation for evolution to work.)

I set my own inward clocks by signs both sensible and insensible: by the time of year, and the thickness of ice on the beaver ponds; by rubs on alders, and the feel of the air. And that day felt like brown trout spawning, and when they spawn, they attack anything that swims near them.

The sun was bright and warm, the air temperature around fifty degrees. That feels warm after a month of getting up before first light and walking through frost after grouse and deer. In early September we'd have worn wool jackets on days like this, but now I wore only a flannel shirt under my fly vest. The body adjusts.

One winter an arctic front came down and kept the temperature below minus-twenty for almost a week. Those were the daytime highs, with lows in the minus-forties, snow and wind mixed in. When the storm broke, the wind died and the sun came out. By nine o'clock, when everyone went to the post office, it was only fourteen below, and many were walking around in flannel shirts and down vests and beatific smiles, telling one another what a nice day it was.

So on this tropical November day I wore my flannel shirt,

though Eileen wore a fleece-lined windbreaker. She also carried a spinning rod, since the wind blew in occasional whirling gusts, picking up cottonwood and alder leaves and spinning them onto the beaver ponds. (That is why she has never gotten really good at fly fishing; unless conditions are perfect she abandons it.) I stuck it out with a big rod, usually reserved for the Missouri.

We entered the river by the gravel bar where Eileen had caught her big rainbow years before. As we stood on the bank a big brown trout squirted up and over the bar, back out of the water. That would happen several times today. They live in three places in November: gravel so shallow nothing but a horny brown trout or a very flat frog would consider it habitable, the tails of pools, and the deep parts of the beaver ponds. They don't move into the ponds until October; before that the water is too warm.

I stepped down into the river itself and another, smaller trout zipped over the gravel bar. I shook my head, looking back at Eileen. She sat on the bank and eased into the water, then dusted the fragments of dry grass from the seat of her jeans.

"You want to try first?" I asked.

She nodded. We walked up along the gravel bar to the undercut bank where I'd caught the big brown. We hadn't caught him since that first time, perhaps because he really listened to my warning and headed some place safer. Very big trout sometimes do that.

But another not-quite-so-big trout had taken his place. He lived during most of the year under an overhanging alder at the head of the undercut. We caught him in spring by drifting a weighted Woolly Bugger, a fly that looks like a caterpillar with a peacock's tail, under the alders, then twitching it. We caught him in midsummer by waiting until dusk and swimming a fly imitating a tiny crayfish through the pool. We caught him in August by drifting a deer-hair grasshopper past the alders or along the undercut. We called him Harvey, because like Jimmy Stewart's rabbit, he was large and reliable.

We caught Harvey in November by standing far back from the undercut and slinging imitation minnows at him. I don't know when we found out that spawning brown trout go nuts over a floating minnow (either lure or deer-hair fly) twitched over their heads, but they do. They come up after it like a bass after a popping bug.

So Eileen stood back and cast carefully toward the deep water just downstream from the alders. The lure landed a little short, so she reeled in and cast again. This time it landed in the center of the pocket, and she turned the reel handle once to close the bail and take in slack line, then gently twitched the lure. It darted a few inches, wobbling once on its side, and the pale bronze side of a trout curved under it in the clear water, a small wave bumping the lure.

"There he is," she said, and twitched it again. And Harvey took it.

The water was too cold for him to jump, but he fought pretty hard. We netted him and the single hook at the rear of the lure fell out of his mouth. Eileen dipped the net into the stream and tilted it forward and Harvey went home.

We'd named him the fall before, after I'd taken a friend out fishing in mid-September and told him where to cast and what size trout he would catch. On his second cast he caught Harvey, right where I said he would. My friend turned to me and asked, "You know them all by name?"

There is some of that on any trout stream you really know. No stream, however, grows quite as predictable as the old story about the aging trout addict who dies and wakes up on the bank of a perfect English chalk stream, a ghillie standing over him, offering a beautiful cane rod.

"There's a good one rising on the far bank, sir," the ghillie says.

The dead angler rises to his feet, much spryer than before he died, and says, "But I can't cast that far."

"Try, sir," the ghillie says, lighting his pipe.

So the dead angler does, dropping the fly just above the rising trout, who takes it. It's a three-pound brown, which jumps once and then fights hard to the net. The ghillie releases it, then says, "There's another rising in the same place, sir."

The angler can't believe it, but casts perfectly again. The trout takes the fly, jumps once, and fights hard to the net, a three-pound brown just like the first one.

"This is amazing!" the angler says.

"Aye, sir," the ghillie says. "There's another one rising."

The angler casts again, catching another three-pound brown. After releasing it, another rises in the same place. The angler, by now sated with three-pound browns, asks if there are any bigger fish in the stream.

The ghillie shrugs. "There may be, sir, but the rules of the river state that you must cast to any rising fish. And there he is." A fish rises in the same place, looking to be another three-pounder.

So the angler casts again, and the fish turns out to be—

surprise—another one-jump three-pounder. After a dozen fish, the angler turns to the ghillie and says, "This doesn't seem much like Heaven to me."

The ghillie lights his pipe again. "Nobody said it was, sir."

Our river never quite became that predictable, despite Harvey. A wild river changes. The beavers came the second year. They built five dams on the mile-long stretch we called our own, changing some holes, widening others, and after another year left. As the dams settled and rotted and washed out, and the bottoms of the pools silted in, the stream changed again each spring.

One year a hot drought persisted from June through early September. Yellowstone Park burned, and the next year all streams were reduced to a two-trout limit. None of the locals who very infrequently fished our stream bothered to show up. "Hell," they said, "It ain't worth buyin' a fishin' license for only two trout." They said this despite the fact that most of them never bought a license in the first place.

We never saw a wader track all summer. The drought hadn't affected the stream at all, and we caught more and bigger fish than we'd ever seen. Harvey seemed average.

Each year we learned a little more about the river, and it came to live on the edges of our minds, always there, like someone you live with and love, almost taken for granted but somehow surprising you every now and then, with reminders of why you love them. A river you live with every day and then, on occasions, want with all your being: a trout stream named desire.

November fishing always seemed like the last days with someone before going on a long trip. So on that day we fished slowly after Eileen caught Harvey, knowing that another good storm would send the fish into semi-hibernation, even if the season lasted until the end of the month. The next pool was a hole below one of the beaver dams, dug during high water when the current fell over the latticed willows. I worked my way upstream along the far bank, shook out some line and roll-cast downstream, then flicked it upstream, the big Muddler Minnow settling onto the still water just below the dam, the leader draped over a willow branch sticking out from the dam. I let the current pull the fly slowly over the branch and it drifted free.

"Good going," Eileen said, standing in the shallow water below the pool.

"Thank you," I said, and twitched the fly. Two trout rolled at it, and when I twitched it again, one chased the other away, then darted back and slashed at the fly. I lifted, and the big Muddler came past my head with a sound like a malevolent insect.

"Good going," Eileen said again.

"I don't think he really had it," I said. I grinned, like a raccoon baring his teeth at headlights. "It warn't my fault, woman."

She smiled. "Never is."

But he hadn't felt the hook, so I cast again and got him, a hard-bodied foot-long trout that I whacked on the head and put in the creel. Then I whacked my hand on the thigh of my wader; holding him was like holding a chunk of ice.

We fished upstream, taking turns at each of the familiar pools. That river has a pool every hundred feet, most built like the pools in instructional trout books. There were hard-turn-under-the-alders pools, cut-bank pools, log pools, and gravel-bar pools. There were the beaver ponds and even some pools not found in texts, though they are common enough in the West: the leaning-barbwire-fence pool, the eroding-buffalo-bones pool, and the '37 Pontiac pool. They all had brown trout, and we caught or turned fish at each one, even catching a couple of rainbows from the beaver ponds.

Then we reached the last barbwire fence, beyond which was another ranch, where we had permission to hunt but not to fish, an odd situation you sometimes run into in eastern Montana. Deer eat haystacks, trout don't. A fox jumped from some rose bushes beside the stream and ran under the fence. The sun was an hour above the mountains.

"I'm cold," Eileen said. She had her jacket zipped up to her nose.

"Yeah, the trout are too." We hadn't turned a fish for twenty minutes. She shoved her hands in her pockets and sat in the sun on top of the bank while I cleaned the three fish we'd kept, two browns and a rainbow. One brown was a female that Eileen had hooked deep; I kept the eggs too, sliding them back into the trout after pulling out the gills and guts. The brown trout male oozed white milt, but the rainbow was sterile, autumnal photoperiod all wrong for his rhythms.

But the sudden cold touched something in us. Light and heat (or lack of it) make wild animals do other things besides reproduce. In squirrels and woodchucks and bears, they bring on a late fall lassitude, the slowing we call hibernation or estivation, according to our own definitions of rhythm.

Whatever. It touched us both. After cleaning the trout and

placing them head to tail in the creel, I lifted my own head, like a bear's. It smelled like winter. To the southwest were hard gray clouds, tight above the mountains. Tomorrow they'd cover most of the sky. Tomorrow, like bears, we'd leave the stream alone. That is what winters are for.

THE LAST
GOOD FISH

You might come here Sunday on a whim. Say
your life broke down. The last good kiss you had
was years ago.

RICHARD HUGO,
"Degrees of Gray in Philipsburg"

The first time I fished the forks of the Popo Agie my life had
not quite broken down, but it might have been Sunday, and as
far as I can remember it was a whim. My first wife and I were
camped up the Middle Fork, above the Sinks, where the river
rides its way into the earth for a distance, then reappears farther down the canyon in a large spring pool. After setting up
the tent, we drove down the canyon to the pool where a sign
said we might throw bread upon the waters so that "Trout of
Enormous Size" could rise up and reveal themselves.

On a bright August day in the Wind River Mountains this

seemed a very fine thing to do, so we unwrapped a peanut butter and jelly sandwich and dissected it into trout food. We leaned on the wooden rail of the deck over the pool and tossed an offering. Perhaps three seconds later a damn big trout angled up through the water, as assured as any fingerling in a stream too small and forgotten for anyone to fish, and took the bread crust in a curve of green.

It had been two years since I'd seen a trout rise, since my wife and I had moved to the midwestern Corn Belt so she could take advantage of a university scholarship. I'd just started fly fishing before we left, and there was a certain westernness in that: I'd killed my first deer when I was thirteen and never caught a trout on a dry fly until I was near twenty. My total fly-rod experience consisted of those fifty airhead grayling and cutthroat in that mountain lake, and another fourteen-inch cutthroat trout that rose to an Adams a friend had given to me when I'd accidentally cast the fly back under the willow where the cutthroat lived. When the trout rose, I struck hard, and he landed in the grass behind me, about as far as an eight-foot fly rod, nine-foot leader, and dozen feet of fly line would allow.

In the past two Midwest years I'd caught bass, catfish, carp, gar, walleye, and pike. I am not a purist. I will gladly canepole for bullheads, especially on a moon-up night with some bacon frying over a driftwood fire and sour mash in a tin cup—and every fish I catch still makes me wonder how we ever got connected. But when I saw that "Trout of Enormous Size" rise in the spring pool of the Sinks, below the cliffs of the Popo Agie's canyon, I remembered the cutthroat rising under willow shadow and felt the last good fish I'd had was years ago.

We got back in the pickup and drove down to the mouth of

the canyon, where we'd passed a sign on an aluminum gate notifying the world that anyone could fish that stretch of the Popo Agie, courtesy of the state of Wyoming. It probably was Sunday, since two other vehicles were in the parking area. I rigged the fly rod I'd been practicing with all summer in our backyard in the Midwest, three blocks from the catfish Missouri.

It is a measure of a certain desperation for anyone to practice fly-casting in public in a corn-country town. Almost every day some high school kids would drive by and holler, "Caught one yet?" One day an old man drove a rusty white pickup into the alley and braked in the dust. He got out and very slowly walked over to me, wearing a baseball cap with a six-inch bill that seemed to lead him forward, like a sail at a boat's bow. He took the fly rod from my hand and cast three times in stiff turn-of-the-century style, as if he had a bible clasped to his ribs with each elbow, then handed the rod back. I cast again, in the long high-arm Lee Wulff sweep, and the old guy angrily shouted "No!" He grabbed the rod again and cast as before, grim-lipped, dipping the bill of his cap rhythmically, like a water ouzel, each dip coinciding with the yarn fly landing on the lawn, before the leader or line. From all my reading I knew this fly-first, bibles-under-the-elbows cast had been highly desirable back in the ancient world, when no one knew how to double haul. So when the old man stopped and offered the rod again, still grim, I planted my elbows in my short ribs and placed the yarn down among the dandelions while the line still floated among the river-bottom mosquitoes. The old man nodded emphatically, then walked to his pickup and drove off, never looking back. He only spoke the one word. I went back to laying sixty feet of line out with long double hauls, occasionally looking furtively over my shoulder for a long-billed cap over the steering wheel of a rusty white truck.

Now I was back in the mountains after two years of corn exile, with a fly rod I could actually cast and perhaps forty trout flies, some the Pride-of-the-Orient specials that Herter's used to sell for $5.63 a gross, some bucktails I'd tied (with all the subtlety of a rodeo roper half-hitching a prone calf), and three #16 Mosquitoes I'd purchased for the extravagant sum of seventy-five cents apiece in a fly shop in Laramie. This was when two could dine sumptuously at almost any roadside cafe for $2.25 and my wife thought briefly of divorce. Several years later we did, the seed perhaps sown by six-bit trout flies.

I rigged the rod but did not put on a fly, since all real fly fisherman, I'd read, looked at what was coming off the water before deciding which piece of artifice in their box might work. We followed a path through alder and cottonwood down to the river—really just a large creek, up there on the edge of the mountains—and found ourselves below a pool, cut by the river half under a low cliff of red sandstone. The water came down from our right, curling and slowing in the shadow of the cliff on the far bank, then sped and flattened into a shallower, wider run where the water ended. I stood there and watched the water. It was midafternoon in August, and even at the mouth of the cool canyon all wise aquatic insects rested under the stones of the Popo Agie.

"Are you fishing for trout?" my wife asked, as if doubting my intent. I nodded. She scratched her chin, looking at the tail of the pool. "Well, there's three or four right there."

I looked and couldn't see anything, then stepped next to her and through the polarized clip-ons over my glasses could see slender green shapes that moved in the water like trailing reeds. Then one of the weeds turned forty-five degrees to the current, and fins flared from its belly. There was a small blink of white at the head, and then the trout became a weed again.

"Well?" she said. "Aren't you going to catch them?" She had grown up with a grandfather—an old Dakota Indian from eastern Montana—who fished a lot. It seemed to her that's what you did: went to a river or lake and then caught fish. It didn't seem fair to tell her that I didn't have much practical experience in catching trout.

But I could see the trout were feeding, even if not rising, so I put on one of my seventy-five-cent flies and rubbed some line dressing on the hackles. Then I backcast three times and caught the fly in an alder, thirty feet behind me and fifteen feet up. "Nice cast," she said.

I tied on another fly and decided to wade into the stream before trying again, keeping my backcast above the water. One small step for man, one clear backcast for mankind. This time I managed to place the fly on top of four trout. "They're pretty nervous now," my wife said.

Here I remembered reading that you should rest spooky trout, so I waited thirty seconds before casting again. This time the fly landed three feet farther upstream, and as it floated down toward me a little splash drowned the fly. I lifted the rod to cast again and there was a trout on the end of the line. He skittered six feet along the surface of the river, reentered the water, then jumped. I ran onto shore and up the bank, stripping line, and the trout bounced over the dry gravel. Even through the layer of dust I could see it was a rainbow, maybe ten inches long. I could not catch another, so we each ate half that evening, in the camp above the Sinks.

We camped up there for quite a while. Actually, we lived up there, since I'd come to town for a new job and we hadn't found a house to rent. So every day she'd drive me down the canyon to Lander and look for a house while I worked. The only available house in our extremely low price range that allowed pets (we had three cats, who'd grown up in a house, and would come running out of the woods and scratch at the tent's door, searching for a cat box) belonged to a woman who was out of town on vacation, according to the bored daughter who answered the phone. So we wrote the absent woman a letter, pleading to get hold of me at my job when she returned, and every day I'd come back from work and catch rainbow trout out of the Middle Fork of the Popo Agie River.

We lived up the Middle Fork for most of a month (come to think of it, maybe there was more to the divorce than three trout flies) before renting that house, moving in just before my wife had to go to Laramie to start graduate school. She would return to Lander after one semester to student-teach on the Wind River Reservation just north of town. In my job, I worked odd shifts and odd stretches, sometimes working two days, then having one off, or eleven days and getting five off. Sometimes I'd drive down to Laramie and see her, and sometimes she came up when I was off, but mostly I lived by myself in a little white house in Lander, worked odd hours at a job I didn't like, and fished the hell out of Wyoming.

It was a long Indian summer that year. In October I caught big spawning brook trout from some beaver ponds on South Pass near Atlantic City, the males so humpbacked I could barely get the first joint of my thumb over their backs when their cool bellies rested on my fingertips, their orange flanks and white-edged fins tropical under the yellow cottonwoods. I fished the North Platte down near the Colorado border one hot midday, casting a Muddler Minnow down along an undercut and seeing a brown "Trout of Enormous Size" ease up from the shadow, just like the rainbow in the Sinks pool. The brown came up behind the Muddler like a hook-jawed kite hovering up from the ground, and when I could not strip the fly in any farther without running it up a riffle, I let it hang there, vibrating in the current. He hung below it, gills flaring lightly like the bellows of a miniature forge. And then he dropped back down into the shadow, as if the breeze holding him there had slowly died.

I fished the lakes in the Winds and the small golden trout streams on the reservation and the ponds out in the middle of the Laramie Valley, encountering the legendary creatures I'd read about in *McClane's Standard Fishing Encylcopedia*— stoneflies and waterboatmen and scuds and caddis. I learned to tie them on small hooks, purchased a dozen at a time from the local sporting goods store with the small amount of money I had left after buying gas for the pickup. On warm October afternoons I would come home tired from the day shift and pick up the *Encyclopedia,* and after reading for fifteen minutes would ask myself: Why read about it? And drive to the forks of the Popo Agie and try to catch a trout.

When I did go to Laramie, I'd plan a route past some place I hadn't fished and then fish again while I was there and visit the fly shop. When my wife came to Lander we'd go up in the Winds or along the Sweetwater on a picnic, and I'd bring the fly rod. In the middle of conversations concerning education, Vietnam, or what to eat for supper, I'd volunteer the information that the Colorado Caddis was the best all-around nymph for central Wyoming. I was in some danger of becoming an aquatic sociopath.

And then it snowed, and I feared my angling life was indeed breaking down—until I looked up the actual closing dates in the Wyoming regulations. There were none. Most of the rivers stayed open all year. I consulted my *Encyclopedia* and then my growing stack of fishing magazines. There were indeed ways to catch trout on flies in the winter. So I kept fishing, like some cold hermit, mostly now on the forks of the Popo Agie since the highways were too icy and days too short to travel much farther. I learned to cast back under the shelves of ice along my favorite pools, to smear line dressing in the guides of my rods to keep ice from building too fast. I learned that after two dozen casts on seventeen-degree days, weighted stonefly nymphs resembled miniature Siberian mammoths encased in layers of ice. The cure was to wrap them in bits of paper towel, place them in a small fly box, then put the fly box in my shirt pocket, under my coat and close to my heart.

In late January the weather dropped below zero for five days in a row, and I found that trout fanatics cannot fish under those conditions since even with a tarpon rod it's hard to cast through ice. The first day after the cold broke I had to work a double shift, and then a morning shift the next day, not getting out to the Middle Fork until an hour before sunset. Warm southwest winds had been blowing for those two days and I knew the big pools would be clear. The rod was already rigged with a weighted stonefly. I pulled on my hip boots quickly and almost ran through the bare alders to the big pool under the red cliff, stripping line out and false-casting as I came from the trees, moving right to the tail of the pool at the stream edge and casting up into the head where the current cut under rock. The white fly line came drifting back, my eyes on the big knot at the base of the leader, and when that knot moved a half-inch, just once, I picked up the rod and stripped in a line and felt a fish, and then saw one turn of paleness in the black pool, as if a mirror had tilted along the bottom. Expecting a whitefish, I was surprised when the mirror twisted nearer and I could see the metal-yellow shape of a good brown trout, as precisely defined as a faceted stone under a jeweler's loupe. The brown pulled hard for the outside of the pool three times, disappearing into the red reflection of the cliff, my rod bent parallel to the shore, before I knelt to take him from the water. As I knelt I realized the fish was much farther below than it should be; I had to stretch out on my belly to get my fingers into the cold water. As I reached for him, he swam under me, underneath what I thought was a sandstone ledge. Looking back and under, grabbing for the evasive trout, I realized it was shelf ice, blown over with red dust, and that I was lying on my belly over the deep edge of the pool on new ice that had been rotting in the warm wind for two days. I grabbed the trout, so much softer than a whitefish, and despite lying there on thin ice, wondered why whitefish were harder than trout and yet fought so softly. Then I crawled back from the edge with my fish, feeling the ice give under the weight of my rod hand, and then realized while sitting back there in the red wet sand that I could not let go of the trout. My hand was too cold. I stood up and knocked the fish against a big alder. It fell out of my hand into the snow under the brush, neck-broken and quivering, and I stuck my frozen hand under my belt and thought: You really are crazy.

A couple of years ago a friend who has fished around the world said, "There is fly fishing for trout, and then there is everything else." He was talking only of fishing, but he said more than he knew. People who do not fish look at it as a rather simple-minded escape—and that is what I tried to make it that winter on the forks of the Popo Agie. If my wife hadn't come back from Laramie, or if I hadn't lain on rotten sand-blown ice, perhaps I could have escaped there.

But fly fishing is not an escape. It is another place in the world, no more or less than some other fine places. It is very comforting, after you have fished hard along a certain stream and know where the trout live in August and October and January and April, to feel it always there. Once you've found that understanding of a river's year, it becomes not just a place to catch trout, but a current with trout in its belly, always running. You do not have to try to find the belly every moment of every day. It's enough to know it is always there. I haven't fished the forks of the Popo Agie for a decade and a half now but still see someone stretched over red ice above a black pool under a cliff, and a pale trout in the center of the pool. The river will always run there, on the border of my life, or another very much like it, full of the last good fish. There is fly fishing for trout, and then there is everything else.